Praying for Our Adult Sons and Daughters

Placing Them in the Heart of God

PRAYING FOR OUR ADULT SONS AND DAUGHTERS

PLACING THEM IN THE HEART OF GOD

John and Therese Boucher

Published by The Word Among Us Press
7115 Guilford Drive
Frederick, Maryland 21704
www.wau.org

20 19 18 17 16   7 8 9 10 11

ISBN:978-1-59325-207-6
eISBN:978-1-59325-440-7

Unless otherwise noted, Scripture passages contained herein
are from the New Revised Standard Version Bible: Catholic Edition,
copyright © 1989, 1993 Division of Christian Education of the National
Council of the Churches of Christ in the United States. All rights reserved.
Used with permission.

Excerpts from the English translation of the *Catechism of the Catholic
Church* for use in the United States of America, copyright © 1994,
United States Catholic Conference, Inc.—Libreria Editrice Vaticana.
Used with permission.

Cover design by John Hamilton Design

Note: All the examples used in this book are based on real-life situations.
Names and identifying details have been altered to ensure confidentiality.

Made and printed in the United States of America

Library of Congress Cataloging-in-Publication Data

Boucher, John J., 1948-
Praying for our adult sons and daughters : placing them in the heart of God
/ John and Therese Boucher.
    p. cm.
Includes bibliographical references.
ISBN 978-1-59325-207-6
1. Parenting—Religious aspects—Catholic Church. 2. Parent and adult
child—Religious aspects--Catholic Church. 3. Parents—Prayers and
devotions. I. Boucher, Therese. II. Title.
BX2352.B68 2012
242'.645--dc23
                                          2012026237

Dedicated to

Connie Reidy

whose constant prayers for her children have
inspired many,

and

David Thorp

who taught hundreds to imagine what God can do
for their grown children.

Contents

INTRODUCTION

At first it didn't seem like a big problem. Barbara's son, Mike, would have a couple of beers after work and a few more on the weekends. He could still hold a job and bring home a paycheck for his young family. But over the last several months, things had gotten worse—much worse. Barbara had prayed in every way possible but had not experienced any answers to her prayers. Finally, her husband suggested a vacation away from the troubling situation.

So off they went to California, where Barbara poured out her heart to God in the San Juan Capistrano chapel. But this time her prayers were different. Instead of crying, she literally lifted up her arms—and her son, Mike—to God. "You take him, Jesus. I give up. He is yours now." Then God's peace flooded her heart. When she arrived home, Barbara learned that on that same day, Mike had gotten into his car and driven to his first AA meeting. By the grace of God, Mike is still going to meetings and has been sober for the past fifteen years.

All of us who are parents have concerns at one time or another about our adult sons and daughters. And that's natural. After all, even though our children are now grown, it wasn't so long ago that we held them in our arms. Remember how good that felt? Just think of all the times you lifted your child from a crib, high chair, or car seat. Once your child became too heavy to lift and hold, you still found ways to cherish him. Maybe he or she sat on your lap or beside you. Still later, you held that child in your heart while providing rides, food, clothing, and homework assistance.

With each act of parenting, a link was forged between you. Even today, that bond is still a part of your own identity, long after your child has reached his twenties, thirties, or forties. And you still want to hold on, even after your grown child has picked up the last box of belongings and carried it out the front door.

God Helps with the "Heavy Lifting"

This is a good desire. But now that our children are adults, we need new strategies for holding on to them, for lifting them up, and for paying attention to them, especially as their needs overwhelm us. We believe that the most important strategy of all is to lift up our adult children in prayer and place them in the heart of God. We do this because our children are God's children first. We also believe that Jesus our Savior is willing to help with the "heavy lifting"! Through him we can raise up our sons and daughters to the Father in prayer. And through prayer, God's love, both for us and for them, is unleashed. We are able to replace our concern with a love that comes from the heart of God. When we lift up our adult sons and daughters and let go, God can move mountains of worry and discouragement. And in their places, God can bring us both refreshment and delight.

In this book, we will encourage you to stop and ask for the Holy Spirit's guidance and to surrender to the new freedom that Jesus wants to give you in prayer. As you do, God's gift of prayer will bring growth in love as well as peace, wisdom, patience, forgiveness, and joy. Your prayers will bring many blessings, seen and unseen. In God's presence, as you experience his gentle love and care, you will be able to face your struggles with difficult feelings like fear and guilt. Your prayer of surrender will become a fruitful tool born of sacrificial love, empowering you to build more successful relationships with your adult daughters and sons. We know, because this has happened to us. Just this past month, we surrendered in prayer our fears about our youngest daughter. As a result, God blessed what could have been a difficult phone call about her finances. Instead, our conversation gave us all a deeper peace about facing her needs.

So take heart. When we pray for grown sons and daughters, God unleashes the gifts and fruits of the Holy Spirit. God intervenes in family life. God offers us new intimacy with our children. God helps us to see our grown children as adult companions on a lifelong journey to heaven. Even if our children are in pain or in danger or if they no longer go to church, God's love for them and for us is without boundaries or limits. As we pray for them in the name of the Father, in the presence of the Son, and in the power of the Holy Spirit, things will happen. God will be present in ways we cannot even imagine.

Expect More of God's Love

Dick is an example of a parent who surrenders in prayer. Every day for about a year, he prayed for his son, Eric, and his daughter-in-law, Carol. Then, during Carol's first pregnancy, he began to focus his prayers on her health. One night he was awakened from a sound sleep with an urgent desire to lift up Carol to God. So he climbed out of bed and prayed for an hour and then went back to sleep. The next morning he called his son, only to discover that the young couple had experienced a miscarriage. It had happened at exactly the time he had climbed out of bed to pray. Dick was in awe as he realized that he had participated in God's compassionate love for his son and daughter-in-law.

Throughout this book, we will meet parents who have prayed for their adult sons and daughters. There's the mother of the sons of Zebedee, who approached Jesus in Matthew's Gospel (20:20). There are canonized parents like St. Elizabeth Seton (1774–1821), who stormed heaven with prayers for the spiritual and moral well-being of her two sons. There are godly parents like Agostino and Stella Cabrini, who raised an ocean-crossing missionary, St. Frances Cabrini (1850–1917), even though they themselves were so afraid to leave their hometown that they failed to collect a sizable inheritance. We have also included ordinary people who use Scripture, the Rosary, the psalms, and even photos to lift up their children to God. Finally, we share our own insights from praying for our five children (whose names have been changed in this book to retain their privacy).

The first five chapters of *Praying for Our Adult Sons and Daughters* explore a parent's prayers for new love, new God-given wisdom, new hope, new Christ-centered forgiveness, and more patient trust about adult children. The next four chapters consider prayers that begin with the needs of a grown son or daughter: for a good spiritual life, for a sense of vocation, for support in times of danger, and for a happiness that endures. The last chapter is about supporting one another as we pray for each other's sons and daughters. Each chapter ends with questions for reflection and instructions for a particular "prayer skill" that promises to help us grow as loving, praying parents.

So let's begin. Let's lift up our grown sons and daughters into the presence of Jesus and into the heart of a loving God. Let's remember that in Jesus, all things are possible. Let's dare to seek more of God's love to give our children. Then let's encourage others to seek more of God's love, not only for their adult sons and daughters, but for their nieces, nephews, and grandchildren as well.

"Ask, and it will be given you; search, and you will find; knock, and the door will be opened to you. . . . Is there any one among you who, if your child asks for a fish, will give a snake instead of a fish? Or if the child asks for an egg, will give a scorpion? If you then, who are evil, know how to give good gifts to your children, how much more will the heavenly Father give the Holy Spirit to those who ask him!" (Luke 11:9, 11-13)

John and Therese Boucher
July 15, 2012
162nd anniversary of the birth of St. Frances Xavier Cabrini

CHAPTER ONE

PRAYING FOR GOD'S LOVE

"It's not like she's fifteen years old," Helen told her friend. "Jennifer is twenty-three now and just got her master's degree in early education, but she waltzed in here with bright pink hair! What was she thinking? How does she expect to get a job or pass an interview? Doesn't she care? I am so disgusted with her right now."

What do you say to a daughter with pink hair or a son who can't hold a job? How do you respond to a thirty-year-old who doesn't see the value of marriage and chooses to live with someone instead? How do you deal with a daughter who isn't bringing her children to be baptized or attend Sunday Mass? How do we let go of our worries and our opinions about their behavior? Where and how do we begin to pray about all this?

We once learned an important lesson about loving grown children from Therese's dad. He was facing yet another surgery during which the doctor would insert yet another dialysis shunt. Therese went with him to the hospital, and together they waited for his turn in the OR. They both knew that every operation at that point in his life was dangerous for him, and so they prayed together. But Therese was very surprised at Dad's prayers. He did not ask God for a successful operation or even for his own survival. He prayed for each of his children by name, asking that each one experience God's love and be drawn ever more deeply into the life of the Church.

God's Love Is Our Beginning Point

I am of the same family as Christ—what more could I want?
—Blessed Pope John XXIII (1881–1963)[1]

For those who believe in Jesus Christ, God's love is our beginning point, our anchor, and the model for every relationship in our families. So when we are driven to the limits of human love, it is the perfect time to approach Jesus in prayer. If we need new strength and wisdom to love a wayward daughter, we can ask Jesus to intervene with his own love and wisdom in that grown child's life. Your most effective strategy as a parent is the same. Enter into God's presence. Lift up your son or daughter to our heavenly Father, whose constant love is beyond our wildest imaginings. The prophet Isaiah gives us a glimpse of the Father's all-encompassing love:

> Do not fear, for I have redeemed you;
>   I have called you by name, you are mine.
> When you pass through the waters, I will be with you;
>   and through the rivers, they shall not overwhelm you;
> when you walk through fire you shall not be burned,
>   and the flame shall not consume you. . . .
> Because you are precious in my sight,
>   and honored, and I love you.
> I give people in return for you,
>   nations in exchange for your life.
> Do not fear, for I am with you. (Isaiah 43:1-2, 4-5)

When you think about your heavenly Father's love for your son or daughter, you only have to think back to your child's spiritual beginnings at Baptism. You presented your son or daughter to God, asking for the waters of new life and the oil of salvation. You sought God's touch upon her ears, eyes, and mouth. You asked that God would bathe your child in light—the light of Jesus, the light of the world. God's life was given on that day. Your child was immersed in the life of the Trinity—the love of the Father, the light of his Son, and the new strength of the Holy Spirit—and not just for a day, or a year, but forever.

When you traced the Sign of the Cross on your little one's forehead, you acknowledged all that God gives through Jesus, our Christ and Lord. It does not matter if this gift has become tarnished and ignored by you or your child. The moment you turn to Jesus and pray on your child's behalf, God hears you. The waters of Baptism are stirred up, and Jesus lavishes his redeeming love on your son or daughter. Every saint who surrounded the font on your child's baptismal day has heard you. Every saint still prays with you for your child. They have not ceased in their affection for your daughter or son. When you pray, all the saints join you, praying that God's love would be poured out on your family.

One day a few years ago, our son Stephen called with a great deal of discouragement in his voice. "I've tried every job I can think of, and this latest one is no better than the others. I want to quit," he declared. We were very concerned and afraid that he was on the verge of a dangerous decision. So later that day, Therese turned to St. John Neumann and asked him to pray. You see, our son Stephen was born on January 5, the feast of St. John Neumann (1811–1860), so we have often asked St. John to pray with us for him. And we were not disappointed. Just a week later, Stephen's sister called home to tell us about an opening for a summer job designing scenery at the theater where she worked. "Do you think Steve might be interested in dropping everything to come?" she asked. God had answered our prayers and pointed Stephen toward carpentry, which eventually became part of his present vocation. More important to us, he has become the happy, thoughtful person he was as a child—God's child and ours.

Prayer Brings New Birth

As parents, we gave life to our children physically, but we can also ask for them to be reborn and renewed spiritually. We asked for Baptism for them as babies, and this choice can be repeated at every step of our child's spiritual and sacramental journey. Through prayer we can return to this important spiritual role as parents. We can step away from our concerns and ask that the gift of baptismal life be unleashed anew by the Holy Spirit. We can ask that God create and recreate a constant life-giving spring in their souls. In Jesus we can even expect that this sacrament will quench the thirst of our sons or daughters. And even if it takes months or years for God to clear away all the debris that impedes the waters of Baptism, God's power is real. Do not lose heart. Pray for the light of Christ to shine once again in your son's or daughter's soul. And do not give up praying.

Now, you might be thinking, "I can't pray like this. I don't even know if God is listening in the first place." But keep this in mind: at your child's Baptism, you also renewed your own baptismal vows. So your child's relationship with God is forever linked to your own Baptism and your own relationship with Jesus. If your spiritual life is lacking, ask for a new outpouring of God's love in your own heart as well as in the heart of your grown child. Place yourself in God's presence. Then speak to Jesus: "Cleanse me, forgive me, renew me, and help me live my own Baptism. Have mercy on me so that I might be an instrument of your love and mercy for each member of my family. Amen."

God's Dream for Us and Our Families

For this reason I bow my knees before the Father, from whom every family in heaven and on earth takes its name. I pray that, according to the riches of his glory, he may grant that you may be strengthened in your inner being with power through his Spirit, and that Christ may dwell in your hearts through faith, as you are being rooted and grounded in love. I pray that you may have the power to comprehend, with all the saints, what is the breadth and length and height and depth, and to know the love of Christ that surpasses knowledge, so that you may be filled with all the fullness of God.

Now to him who by the power at work within us is able to accomplish abundantly far more than all we can ask or imagine, to him be glory in the church and in Christ Jesus to all generations, forever and ever. Amen. (Ephesians 3:14-21)

St. Paul's Letter to the Ephesians describes God's love for us and how his life is meant to unfold among us. Above all, God promises new life for all the baptized, for you and for your family.

So seek God's life by pursuing a vision of family life where all are formed and re-formed in the likeness of Jesus. Seek Christ in every way possible. Seek the Holy Spirit as a spiritual compass pointing toward the immeasurable goodness of God and his presence in your family. Pray with St. Paul. Lay down your innermost being, your relationships, all of your joys, and especially your sorrows, at the feet of Jesus. At the heart of God's love is a Trinity of relationships, drawing us in and drawing us together.

Even when you're not sure of God's love for a particular family member, Christ dwells in you. Even when you pray through tears, you can choose to cry those tears in the presence of Jesus. He is the key to understanding the breadth and depth of God's love. We can be certain of this because, in the words of Psalm 34, "The LORD is near to those who are discouraged; / he saves those who have lost all hope (verse 18, Today's English Version). And finally, whether you are afraid or unafraid, seek the Holy Spirit, asking to become more rooted and grounded in God's love for your family. Then through the Spirit, God will help you in new ways.

Ben was always watching for signs of God's presence in his daughter's life. One afternoon just before a ministry meeting, he leaned over to tell John what his daughter, Denise, had written on Facebook: "It's my thirtieth birthday, and it's raining here in San Diego. It never rains here. Never! I think the rain is God crying for my lost youth." Ben was thrilled. "She referenced God!" he said. "Maybe she is not as much of an atheist as we thought!" Ben took this as a small glimmer of hope, one that would sustain him for weeks to come.

Not only does God love us beyond all imagining, but Jesus loves us so much that he intercedes for us before the Father.

David had a striking realization of this truth while handing out tickets to his children at an amusement park. A little boy standing behind his fifth child put his hand out for a ticket. David was indignant. "I spend enough money on my own kids!" he thought. But the little boy persisted, and David heard his son cry out, "Dad, this is my friend. I told him you would give him a ticket!" David was stunned. "This same thing happens when I ask our heavenly Father to give me what I need, when I ask in the name of his beloved Son, Jesus, who is also my friend." So when is the last time you asked Jesus for a son's or daughter's ticket to heaven? Do you trust that Jesus will intercede for you before his heavenly Father?

Surrender All to God's Love

When we share in God's saving love, we understand that *every need* can become the object of petition. Christ, who assumed all things in order to redeem all things, is glorified by what we ask the Father in his name. It is with this confidence that St. James and St. Paul exhort us to pray *at all times*. (CCC 2633)

When we ask our Father for what our grown children need, we join ourselves to Jesus, who intercedes at the right hand of the Father. But at the same time, we also stand on the threshold of a spiritual contradiction. On the one hand, Jesus encourages us to go to the Father with all of our needs. On the other hand, he exhorts us to have faith and stop worrying. Perhaps the answer to this puzzle lies in praying *through* our worries, no matter how long it takes to experience relief. Perhaps the answer lies in finding a way to get "unstuck" in prayer, a way to see things from God's point of view.

John remembers spending many years begging God to help him earn enough money to send our last two children to college. "How can I supplement my church salary, pay our massive medical bills, and still send them to college?" he asked in prayer. Then one day he asked his spiritual director for help. She told him, "Write down the amounts that each of your three older children received in scholarships." He did. "Now add them up." And he did. "Could you have earned all of that money with a better paying job?" The answer was a clear and resounding "No!"

His struggle illustrates that praying for a grown child's needs can be a messy proposition. Such prayer might take a long time. It might involve sorting through many emotions. It might even require the support of others, such as counselors or spiritual directors. But the good news is that in John's case, bringing his fears to his spiritual director helped him realize God's love for him as a provider and for all of our graduating children.

So turn away from worry, depression, and fear. Turn toward God, and take the time to describe your grown child's or children's needs as part of your daily prayers. And be sure to include your own feelings about their needs. If you have several grown children, you may want to pray for each of them by name every day, but then spend a little more time praying for just one of them. Then the next day, pray for the next son or daughter. In this way, you will give spiritual attention to each one over the course of a week. And finally, keep in mind that God already knows what each one needs. So you can pray, "Jesus, remember what I asked for yesterday? I believe that you have already heard my prayer and are working on an answer. You know what is needed. You care about her (or his) troubles. So I give my daughter (or son) to you again. I place my child in your care right now, most holy Savior. Amen."

Saintly Parents Pray

There are many encouraging scriptural examples of parents who lifted up their children to God in prayer. The greatest of these is Mary, the mother of Jesus, who pondered both the glorious song of the angels on Christmas morning and the message of the prophets Simeon and Anna in the Temple. "Then Simeon blessed them and said to his mother Mary, 'This child is destined for the falling and the rising of many in Israel, . . . so that the inner thoughts of many will be revealed—and a sword will pierce your own soul too'" (Luke 2:34, 35).

Imagine how many times Mary turned to God in prayer about her son, Jesus. Imagine her agonizing prayers on the day that John the Baptist, the son of her kinswoman Elizabeth, was murdered. Think about how she prayed for Jesus when he argued with the Pharisees or got jostled by large crowds. How did she pray during their last and most dangerous journey to Jerusalem? What were her prayers when Jesus was convicted as a common criminal? And what kind of prayer gave her the courage to stand by Jesus at the foot of the cross? We can only imagine. But if we imitate Mary's constancy in prayer, then we, too, will have the courage and the humility to stand as a healing presence beside our children when they face their own crosses.

Another example of a praying parent is Blessed Marie of the Incarnation (1599–1672). After her husband's death, she left

France and her eleven-year-old son, Claude, to become an Ursuline missionary in Quebec. She and her son missed each other terribly. But she placed him in God's care and surrendered him and herself to God's will often. We get a glimpse of her prayerful affection in their letters. In 1643, for example, Claude wrote to Marie, telling her that he had taken his vows as a Benedictine priest. When he asked if he would ever see her again, Marie responded, "Let us leave it to God. I should wish for it as much as you, but I wish to wish for nothing except in Him and for Him; let us lose our own wills for His love." And again in 1651, she wrote, "God has wonderful treasures of goodness for simple souls who trust themselves to Him. You must believe that we have a God who cared for us in every minute of the past, and who will continue to do so in the future."[2] Then, finally, as she lay dying, surrounded by her beloved Algonquin orphans, she told her sisters to write to Claude and tell him that she would carry him in her heart on her journey to heaven.

The Sacrifice of Thanksgiving

God calls us to surrender our lives and the lives of our grown sons and daughters in prayer. When we do so, we offer God one of the most meaningful sacrifices of all. We lift up our children from the depths of our hearts and place them in God's heart. We step aside from our feelings and step away from loving them alone. We become like Blessed Marie, or Abraham, willing to let go of our own flesh and blood for the sake of God's love. This means letting go of a person who has been an intimate part of our lives physically, emotionally, and spiritually. It means sacrificing not only a son or daughter, but the years spent providing for them. For all of us, prayerful surrender acknowledges God as the ultimate source of all goodness and hope. God alone can love our children, through us or in spite of us.

Gratitude is another step each parent can take in the presence of God. It does not matter what your grown child is facing or what is happening in your relationship with an offspring. What matters is God's invitation to look at your child with a thankful heart. So begin your prayers by slowly breathing in God's Holy Spirit for a few moments. Then lift up your grown child to God by raising your arms to heaven. Thank the Father for every good thing about your child. Start small if you have to: "Thank you for his smile and those blue, blue eyes. Thank you for his affection for his children. Thank you for his gifts. I even thank you for showing me his pain." Then tell God about that son's or daughter's needs as well.

Thank God Ahead of Time

Venerable Solanus Casey, OFM Cap (1870–1956), the first American-born male candidate for sainthood, encouraged many to pray in radical gratefulness. He would instruct each person to thank Jesus ahead of time for God's response, "leaving everything at His divine disposal, [up to and] including all [the details] . . . of our death."[3] Jean embraced Solanus' message of prayerful gratitude when her single thirty-year-old daughter, Peggy, gave birth while in medical school. She thanked God during her own struggle with serious health problems, even when her illness prohibited her from babysitting Peggy's newborn. She wrote to Therese, "It is impossible to say that nothing more could go wrong. But I am so glad that you and John introduced me to Fr. Solanus Casey. I have been thanking God ahead of time for more than three months now. He has been so faithful and merciful to my daughter and her baby." Still later, we were amazed at God's timing. Peggy finished her final exams the night before Jean was hospitalized with a critical illness. So Peggy was free to rush to her mother's bedside.

When we thank God, like Jean and Solanus, we move from problem-centered petitions to God-centered worship. We imitate the psalms of lament that move from tribulations to seeking God's point of view and voicing an expression of hope. A good example is Psalm 22, which Jesus prayed on the cross. Let us imitate the psalmist and Jesus and move toward thanksgiving for our grown children. Let us move toward God's heart.

As in the prayer of petition, every event and need can become an offering of thanksgiving. The letters of St. Paul often begin and end with thanksgiving, and the Lord Jesus is always present in it: "Give thanks in all circumstances; for this is the will of God in Christ Jesus for you" (1 Thessalonians 5:18); "Continue steadfastly in prayer, being watchful in it with thanksgiving" (Colossians 4:2). (CCC 2638)

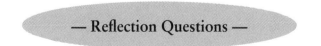

— Reflection Questions —

1. What is your understanding of prayer? What has been your experience of praying for your grown children? In what ways has praying for them influenced your life or theirs?

2. What do you remember of your child's Baptism? What did this event mean to you and to your family at that time? What meaning does it have for you now?

3. What was it like when your grown child came of age and moved on to his or her own life? How could you grow in respect for this grown child as an adult? What comes to mind when you hear about letting go and surrendering this son or daughter to God?

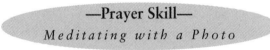

—Prayer Skill—
Meditating with a Photo

Many of us think in pictures instead of words. Visual prayer can unleash our imaginations and bring richer encounters with God. One way to pray visually is to use family photos. We first heard about this idea from one father whose college-aged son was in trouble. "I prayed with a picture of him when he was about seven—in other words, when he was cute. Before long I found myself thanking God for his good qualities and leaving the rest behind." So try praying with a photo. Pray beyond words, and explore the refreshing currency of hands, eyes, and nonverbal realities.

Choose a photo of one grown child and sit in your normal prayer place. Choosing only one son or daughter will help you focus on God's particular and unique love for that child. (We will guide you through praying with a group photo later.) If you do not have a photo, use one of that child's belongings or a gift that they gave you.

Opening Prayer: He [Jesus] is the image of the invisible God, the firstborn of all creation; for in him all things in heaven and on earth were created, things visible and invisible, . . . all things have been created through him and for him. He himself is before all things, and in him all things hold together. (Colossians 1:15-17)

Lord Jesus, my Savior and brother, when I look at this photo, I am _____.

(If you don't know what to say, simply tell God your feelings, sing a hymn, or just repeat the name of Jesus while looking at the photo.)

Holy Father, I believe that you love my child, _____ *(name)*. I choose your blessings for her/him now. And I ask your forgiveness for my sins against _____ *(name)*.

(Trace the Sign of the Cross over the photo, then lift the photo up as a way of offering your child to God.)

Thank you for giving me _____ *(name)*.

Ending Prayer: Father in heaven, you made each of us in the likeness of your Son, and you sent your Spirit to restore us in his image. Touch the heart of my loved one with your merciful love. Use me as a source of blessing, forgiveness, and peace. Send me, or someone of your choosing, as a witness of your good news and joy for my son/daughter. I ask this through Christ our Lord. Amen.

CHAPTER TWO

PRAYING FOR WISDOM

At one time, our oldest son, Charlie, went through a very painful divorce. His grief and anger were so intense that they washed over our family like a tsunami. For several months, John listened to Charlie in lengthy phone calls and e-mails. John tried to reflect back to Charlie what he heard him saying. Then, during a difficult conversation, our son started blaming us for his divorce. He reasoned that our thirty-plus years as a faith-filled married couple had given him an unrealistic view of marriage. Somehow we had messed up his life! That's when John lost it.

"How can you blame us for your choices? Take responsibility for your own decisions. You're an adult. For God's sake, get some counseling!" With these few words, John crossed the line from listening to giving unsolicited advice. Charlie was so furious that he wouldn't talk to John for nearly two years. He also stopped coming to family gatherings at Thanksgiving and Christmas.

For a long time after this, John felt as if he had failed as a parent. So he began to pray differently: "Lord Jesus, help Charlie. Be with him. Send your Holy Spirit to both of us, and keep me from saying or doing anything stupid! Give me your wisdom so that I can rise above my own doubts. Help me know what to say or not say. Help me know what to do or not do. Let your Spirit shape my thinking so that I might love the way you love." John prayed this way for a very long time, and he and Charlie eventually reconciled. He still prays this way today, especially when one of our adult children faces difficulties that John doesn't understand.

Seeking God's Wisdom

If any of you is lacking in wisdom, ask God, who gives to all generously and ungrudgingly, and it will be given to you. But ask in faith, never doubting, for the one who doubts is like a wave of the sea, driven and tossed by the wind. (James 1:5-6)

In this chapter, we will consider ways to seek wisdom in prayer. An important first step is realizing that when we seek God's wisdom, we are not seeking a complicated solution to a puzzle. We are seeking the Person of the Holy Spirit. We are searching for God's vision of our sons and daughters. So we persevere in surrendering our minds and hearts to the Holy Spirit, who is an ever-abundant font of truth and understanding. We call upon the Holy Spirit, who is "the Lord, the giver of life." We seek the Holy Spirit, who can fill us, surround us, enlighten us, and drench us in God's love. Then we ask that through our prayers, God's creative love will be showered on our sons and daughters, on our families, and ultimately upon all of humanity.

As the *Catechism* tells us, "With creation God does not abandon his creatures to themselves. He not only gives them being and existence, but also, and at every moment, upholds and sustains them in being, enables them to act and brings them to their final end," which is God himself. "Recognizing this utter dependence with respect to the Creator is a source of wisdom and freedom, of joy and confidence" (CCC 301).

When we surrender to the Spirit's wisdom, we acknowledge this Person, whose sustaining presence and guidance unfolds as we persist in prayer. We may begin with a jumble of questions and concerns, but we lift up each question to God as a way of giving over our children's lives to him. We seek the Holy Spirit as a faithful companion, an advocate, and a friend who offers us peace, patience, faithfulness, self-control, and even joy. We seek the Spirit as a guide and teacher who empowers us for this essential spiritual role that is part of our vocation as parents. We seek the Holy Spirit as an intercessor, for us and within us on behalf of our sons and daughters. We seek and find the Holy Spirit, who is hope and light.

God's Ongoing Guidance though Jesus

Our prayers for wisdom are part of a larger search for God's covenant love that first began with two very important parents, Abraham and Sarah (Genesis 12 to 25). They did not know all the details about their future family, but they had the wisdom to rely on God's promises and move forward. Imagine what it was like for Abraham to seek God's wisdom about sacrificing his son, Isaac. Did God want Abraham to surrender his son or not? Abraham's question ended in a new and better understanding of God's covenant love for his family and for every believing parent who would come after him, all the way down to New Testament times, when that covenant love took flesh in the Person of Jesus. How fortunate we are that God's greatest wisdom can now be found in Jesus! So let the Spirit lead you. As St. Francis de Sales (1567–1622) wrote, "As often as you can throughout the day, recall your mind into the presence of God. Consider what God is doing and what you are doing. You will always find God's eyes fixed upon you with unchangeable love."

The Holy Spirit also helps us recognize and follow the voice of Jesus, who wants to guide us. Through the Spirit, our eyes are opened to Jesus as shepherd, healer, teacher, and redeemer in our daily lives and in the lives of our children. We gain a new respect for the unique call that each of us has to live a personal and communal relationship with Jesus Christ. The gifts of wisdom and understanding become a part of the fabric of our day-to-day lives as energetic disciples of Jesus our Lord. Finally, through the Holy Spirit, we seek wisdom in the Bible, solace in celebrating the sacraments, and strength in the gatherings of the Christian community. And it is in this context that we learn new ways to love, speak, and act toward our grown children and families.

So even when you are in the middle of an uncomfortable and distressing experience and you don't think you have all the answers, resist the temptation to think that God has no answers for you. Don't give up. Let the Spirit guide you toward the wisdom you need about parenting adults. Seek help in the Church. The fullness of wisdom resides in the whole Church as a gift. Your uncertainty is a normal stepping-stone to an even deeper surrender to the Holy Spirit and a richer life as a follower of Jesus within the body of Christ. We can make this prayer of Blessed Charles de Foucauld (1858–1916) our own:

Father, I abandon myself into Your hands; do with me what you will. Whatever you may do, I thank you: I am ready for all, I accept all. Let only Your will be done in me and in all Your creatures—I wish no more than this, Lord.[4]

Surrendering to the Holy Spirit

We suggest the following steps for seeking the wisdom of the Holy Spirit. It is never too early or too late to seek God's wisdom about a son's or daughter's difficulties or needs. This kind of prayer unleashes God's power in ways we don't always understand, any more than we understand how electricity works. We need to connect ourselves to the power of God's love often, even when we don't see results. And we need to work at making Jesus Christ the Lord of our lives, the Lord of our worries.

First, ask the Father to intervene in a son's or daughter's life, especially if their situation is not in line with the message of God's love and our redemption in Jesus. The Father is concerned about their well-being and will respond. Ask God to show you how he is already at work in their situation.

Second, ask God to send the Holy Spirit into their lives as a guide. Ask for the help they need to recognize God's guidance.

Third, ask for the gift of understanding. Let go of your opinions and your desires to solve their problems. Our goal is to offer up our children to God and let Jesus do the "heavy lifting." It is a rare adult son or daughter who can accept a parent's unsolicited advice without feeling threatened.

Fourth, ask for God's help in choosing just one detail to pray about. We must let go of knowing God's whole plan for a loved one's life, because their needs can easily get tangled up with our own.

Fifth, speak in ways that affirm your son or daughter. Ask respectful questions that will give you better understanding, such as "Could you tell me more about . . . ?" or "Have you ever thought about . . . ?" Act or serve in ways that reflect God's love and that utilize the fruits of the Holy Spirit—peace, joy, patience, and understanding. These fruits of the Spirit may not always come naturally; you will need practice.

An Example of Surrender Prayer

Let's follow our friend Russ through these steps for seeking God's wisdom. At one time, his daughter, Alice, fled her home with her young son, Jeffrey, because her alcoholic husband had become verbally and physically abusive. Of course, Russ's first prayer was for the safety of his daughter and grandchild. But after the immediate crisis had passed, Russ had no idea how to pray for her. "Should I pray that her husband, Howard, enter a twelve-step program?" he wondered. "Should I beg Jesus for reconciliation between them? Should I pray that Alice have the strength to divorce him? Show me how to pray my way through this mess."

Step One: Watching for God's intervention was difficult for Russ. He prayed, "God, show me how you are *already* working." Then he reexamined the events of the previous week. As he did, Russ began to thank Jesus that Alice and Jeffrey were now living in safe emergency housing and that Howard had been given a chance to face his behavior and had already received family encouragement to get help.

Steps Two and Three: Russ asked the Holy Spirit to help his daughter know what to do next. "Send her someone who will befriend her in the ways that she needs. Send her good advisors. I offer her to you. I offer myself to you and then to her in the ways that you show me." He also began reading a book about alcoholism and its effects on family life.

Step Four: Russ prayed, "I need your wisdom about how to pray, Jesus. Show me one specific thing I can pray for." Then after talking with his daughter, Russ began to pray for a more permanent living situation for Alice. At first it seemed as though God wasn't listening. Alice's finances presented a huge roadblock to renting. But after a few weeks, God intervened through some good friends. They invited Alice and Jeffrey to move into their oversized spare room. It was just what Alice and her son needed. So Russ was free to move on to praying for the next thing that God would show him.

Step Five: The next time Russ spoke with Alice, he said, "Wow! God must really love you to give you such good friends." Then he rearranged his schedule so that he could visit his daughter, affirm her choice of a new home, and thank Alice's friends in person.

> We know that all things work together for good for those who love God, who are called according to his purpose. (Romans 8:28)

When you pray with an eye toward God's step-by-step plan, you will become more confident about the Father's ongoing care for your sons and daughters. You will realize that the Spirit of God is working even before you realize the need to ask. No matter how far your children might be from God or from the Church, you will begin to see the Holy Spirit working to change their hearts or to change situations that keep them from his love.

If you don't see results, and if God's love for a son or daughter seems to be invisible, resist the temptation to stop praying. Instead, you may want to intensify your prayer by dedicating yourself to spending more time in daily prayer, to a day-long retreat, to daily Mass, or to sacrifices like fasting. Any of these additional prayer decisions can be avenues for acting out your belief in the Holy Spirit, who is the heart and soul of prayer.

Change Me First, God

When you have taken steps to seek God's ongoing wisdom about your adult children and are still feeling anxious, driven to tears, or ranting in anger, then it is time to consider another crucial part of seeking God's wisdom: you cannot change your daughter or son—you can only change yourself! Give God a blank check. Surrender your whole life to God for the sake of your adult child:

I appeal to you therefore, brothers and sisters, by the mercies of God, to present your bodies as a living sacrifice, holy and acceptable to God, which is your spiritual worship. Do not be conformed to this world, but be transformed by the renewing of your minds, so that you may discern what is the will of God—what is good and acceptable and perfect. (Romans 12:1-2)

It is part of God's loving plan to change you and to remove any obstacles to your receiving the sanctifying gifts of the Holy Spirit—like wisdom, fortitude, and counsel. Ask God to unlock these gifts so that you can see your son or daughter from God's point of view, and then respond accordingly. These sanctifying gifts were already given to you through the sacraments of initiation (Baptism, Eucharist, and Confirmation). Ask God to bring them to fruition. Ask for a new responsiveness to the prompting of the Spirit, which will enable you to use these sanctifying gifts in daily life.

In Russ's case, he refrained from a knee-jerk reaction to drive six hundred miles to Alice's house. Instead, he prayed for an increase in the Spirit's gift of counsel so that he could assist Alice in handling her own life as an adult. Then he focused his prayer on Alice's need for a place to live. After that prayer was answered, he asked for gifts of patience and fortitude so that he could support his wife as she spoke with their daughter several times each week. All these steps were ways of giving God room to answer his prayers. "God guides all by the action of His grace," wrote St. Anthony the Great (c. 251–356). "Therefore do not be lazy or lose heart, but call to God day and night to entreat [him] to send you help from above to teach you what to do."[5]

God's Wisdom Is Creative

At one time, John sought God's wisdom about our son Stephen, who is quite introverted and was unsure about making a move to a new city. John was uncomfortable with reaching out by way of more phone calls. So he asked God to change his feelings or to change the situation. A few weeks later, Stephen invited John to play chess online. The program offered a "chat box" where each one could write a short message after making a move. John recognized this God-given opportunity and decided that he would also take the time after each move to jot down a few words about what he was doing and about Stephen's latest job assignments. Now we can say that for the first time since Stephen went off to college, John and Stephen have an ongoing adult relationship, and John has a new appreciation for Stephen's unique stance toward life.

John also finds it helpful to refer back to his earliest experiences of God's creative guidance, which happened while he was teaching our teenagers how to drive. Each one had problems with a different driving skill. One found making turns to be challenging; another had trouble looking far enough ahead. One found backing up to be a death-defying act; another wrestled with parallel parking. Every time he took one of our teenagers out to drive, he would write in his spiritual journal about the experience. He began with complaints about their mistakes but then would repent of his own responses. Over time, daily journaling helped him to realize that our teenagers would soon become adults and fellow drivers. So he decided to prepare for each lesson by thanking God for the confident and skillful drivers that they would become.

Both then and now, he realizes that those driving lessons were actually spiritual exercises for him. They were practice in letting go of our teenagers as drivers and as fledgling adults with their own approaches—pluses and minuses—in facing life.

Receiving and Sharing Wisdom Take Time

Prayer for wisdom implies admitting that each of us is a work in progress. It implies revisiting what we believe and what we think. It means starting all over again in the light of important things that are happening around us. Prayer for wisdom implies being shaped and reshaped. It implies being lost and found and lost again. To grow in wisdom is to engage in a kind of waltz with God that moves us through many surrender moments. St. Ignatius Loyola (1491–1556) wrote this famous prayer about surrendering all to be guided by God's will:

Lord Jesus Christ, take all my freedom,
my memory, my understanding, and my will.
All that I have and cherish
You have given me.
I surrender it all to be guided by Your will.
Your grace and Your love
are enough for me.
Give me these, Lord Jesus,
and I ask for nothing more.

Praying for God's wisdom is not like using a vending machine or clicking on a web-page link. There is no magic amount of prayer, learning, or sacrifice that will solve our grown children's problems or instantly inspire our grown children to marry in the Church, leave an addiction behind, or forsake one of a dozen dangerous activities. But we can be confident that the Holy Spirit is already acting in their lives, known or unknown to them and to us. We can pray about the next step in our mutual journey toward God, expecting God to reveal himself to them and to us.

We also humbly seek and accept wisdom as a mutual gift that we share with our adult sons and daughters. And we can acknowledge this gift by asking their advice about the issues and decisions that we face in our own lives. In our case, we appreciated the insights that our older children offered about decisions we needed to make about our fifth child, Rose, when she was in college. Because the three oldest were born fourteen to seventeen years before Rose, they had an important and more current understanding of her situation than we did. With their help, we felt much more confident as we lifted up Rose to Jesus and lifted up our own lives as older parents.

So we encourage each of you to rely on the Holy Spirit, who will help all of us as parents in countless ways as we trust in him. "Cast yourself into the arms of God and be very sure that if He wants anything of you, He will fit you for the work and give you strength," wrote St. Philip Neri (1515–1595). We invite you to take heart from the "O Antiphons" used during Advent that help us wait during the last days before Christmas. These seven prayers have been in use since the ninth century and are sung or spoken as Gospel acclamations during the week before the birth of Jesus Christ. They underscore the perennial importance of seeking ongoing wisdom from God. The very first of these antiphons sets the stage for successful waiting by addressing the Holy Spirit, and so we paraphrase: "O Wisdom, voice of the Most High God, orchestrating everything in all of creation by your mere presence, teach us your ways."

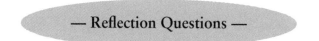

— Reflection Questions —

1. What are your experiences of watching adult sons and daughters struggle with decisions? What role do you find yourself taking in your concern for them? What does it mean to parent a grown child in this type of situation?

2. What is your relationship with the Holy Spirit like? What sources do you rely on for wisdom? What more could you do to seek God's wisdom about a son or daughter or about your own life?

3. How is your adult child an "adult companion" in your life, capable of providing mutual support and offering wisdom? What might you do to make your relationship more respectful of him or her?

—Prayer Skill—
Journaling God's Love for My Child

Ever get locked out of your car—totally locked out, without even a spare wallet key? That's what prayer is like without the Holy Spirit: there is no way to move forward. When we feel stalled in prayer, spiritual journaling can help, because a notebook becomes a spiritual road map of the day-to-day guidance of the Holy Spirit. The act of writing—regardless of spelling errors or messy handwriting—illuminates areas of our lives that need the transforming touch of the Holy Spirit.

Step One: Slowly pray, "Come, Holy Spirit. Fill my heart that I might see and reflect the love of Jesus for my children. Show me how he has been present to them." Then slowly read this passage until a word, phrase, or verse strikes you:

> I lift up my eyes to the hills—
> from where will my help come?
> My help comes from the LORD,
> who made heaven and earth. . . .
>
> The LORD will keep you from all evil;
> he will keep your life.
> The LORD will keep
> your going out and your coming in
> from this time on and forevermore.
> (Psalm 121:1-2, 7-8)

Step Two: List a few major events in your grown child's life—birth, an important school experience, graduation, marriage, or an adult achievement. Choose one event to write about. How was your son or daughter created, re-created, or sustained by God at this time? What evidence do you have that Jesus was present in this event? What hope does this passage From Psalm 121 offer you about the future?

Step Three: End with a statement about your belief in God's love or a prayer to God the Holy Spirit. (This can be verbal or written.)

> O Holy Spirit, O Living water,
> wash me in your cleansing streams.
> O Holy Spirit, O Living fire,
> enkindle in me the flames of your passionate love for others.
> O Holy Spirit, O Breath of God,
> bear me up on the wings of peace;
> O Holy Spirit,
> I wish to be swept away by the embrace of your abiding presence. Amen.

CHAPTER THREE

PRAYING FOR HOPEFUL ACCEPTANCE

We were delighted when we heard that our daughter Claire and her husband were expecting their first son. It didn't take long for them to choose "Derek" as his first name, but his middle name was a different story. Claire wanted the name "Harry," after Therese's dad, while her husband, Bruce, wanted the name "Nolan," after a favorite baseball player. The discussion continued all the way into the labor room. It was very tempting to take sides. But after a lot of prayer, God gave us the grace to keep quiet and accept their choice. After all, Claire and Bruce's dreams for their son should prevail over ours.

When our daughters and sons face hopeful events like the birth of a baby, a wedding, or a new job, our hopes and dreams for them surface like bubbles in champagne. It is easy to celebrate God's loving presence with joyful hymns and prayers of thanksgiving. But when they face distressing events like death or divorce, a parent's hopes and dreams take a real beating. The dangers they face in their lives can shatter our hopes and dreams for them into a million pieces. In addition, any major event can precipitate a conflict between our grown children's dreams and our own dreams for them. So how do we pray in these situations? How do we move from our broken or threatened dreams into hopeful acceptance? St. Pio of Pietrelcina (1887–1968) gives us a good starting point.

Pray, hope, and don't worry! Worry is useless. God is merciful and will hear your prayer. Prayer is the best weapon we have; it is the key to God's heart. You must speak to Jesus not only with your lips but with your heart. In fact, on certain occasions, you should speak to Him only with your heart.

Lifting Up Our Hearts' Desires to Jesus

An essential beginning point for hopeful acceptance is honesty about our heart's desires and deepest longings. Like the mother of the sons of Zebedee, who asked Jesus to grant her two sons choice positions in his kingdom (Matthew 20:20), we must admit what we want most for our children. We must give God all the emotions behind our desires, no matter how messy our prayers become. For it is in doing so that the Holy Spirit will help us sort out and identify our unfulfilled dreams, a grown child's dreams, and God's hopes for that child. Our friend Lorraine shares her hopes and dreams as she prays for her adult children.

For those who live nearby or right under my nose, I just ask God to take care of their everyday needs and their little dreams. For instance, Melanie doesn't have a boyfriend right now, so I pray that she meets someone good today, someone I could enjoy too. For those who live far away and often rely only on texting or leaving cryptic comments on Facebook to communicate, I fall back on the dreams that I had for them when they were little children. I use the blessing prayers that I taught them. I pray that they be happy and healthy, that they be good and kind, and that they be responsible and wise. And I pray that they know God, love God, and walk in his ways today. Those are my dreams for them.

Phyllis honestly faced her dreams and desires for her daughter, Jodie, when she received an unexpected phone call from her one day. "I didn't want to admit to you how horrible our finances are," Jodie said. "But tomorrow we have an appointment in bankruptcy court, and none of our friends or neighbors can babysit for us. Can you come?" Of course, Phyllis dropped everything and left. As she packed her bag, her mind raced through a barrage of frightening questions. Would the house that Jodie and her husband had purchased go into foreclosure? Would the children lose their private schooling? Would Jodie have enough money for gas and her long commute to work? Would they have enough money for food? How many dreams for Jodie would she have to forgo? Phyllis made two copies of a list of worries: one to place at the feet of her favorite Sacred Heart statue, and the other for the long bus ride. She would surrender each concern, one by one, in prayer.

When dreams about the future are in jeopardy, we might feel like anxious, twittering birds on a high-tension wire getting hit with rushing volts of electricity. We might feel like a thirsty, panting deer in desperate need of live-giving water (Psalm 42:2-3). We might function like a woman in labor, all wrapped up in endless agonizing pain. Honest prayer can be so difficult that we want to avoid it, but we can trust God. Jesus is a physician, a friend, and a confidant. Nothing is impossible with God's help.

Dream in God's Presence

We know that the whole creation has been groaning in labor pains until now; and not only the creation, but we ourselves, who have the first fruits of the Spirit, groan inwardly while we wait. . . . Likewise the Spirit helps us in our weakness; for we do not know how to pray as we ought, but that very Spirit intercedes with sighs too deep for words. (Romans 8:22-23, 26)

Prayer is sacrifice. Prayer is being honest with ourselves about our own dreams and desires for our children, and then giving ourselves and those desires to God in the present moment. Even if we pray with sighs, groans, tears, or unexplainable emotions, the key to facing the future is praying in the moment, sacrificing our dreams and surrendering them to God.

Therese recalls being in the labor room with our daughter Ann when the baby was in distress. "Help, God! Help! Help! Holy Father, save this child!" was Therese's prayer. Getting beyond this kind of prayer did not seem possible. Then her own sister, Susan, called to share a dream about their dad covering the baby with his deacon vestments. Therese was then able to pray, "I accept all that you are doing and all that you want to do for Ann and the baby. They are yours, God, not mine." In the peace that followed, Therese was able to support Ann and her husband. God granted two miracles: Therese's surrender in prayer and the successful delivery of our little grandson, despite the fact that the umbilical cord had been wrapped around his neck.

A scriptural example involves the relationship between Jesus and his close friend Lazarus. They enjoyed each other's company often. And then, just when Jesus needed him most, Lazarus developed a terminal illness. Imagine Jesus praying to his Father and surrendering his dreams about his visits with Lazarus and their friendship. The Father honored the sacrifice of those dreams, which we realize when we listen to Jesus explaining the death of his friend: "This illness does not lead to death; rather it is for God's glory, so that the Son of God may be glorified through it" (John 11:4).

God's Wildest Dreams

When we sacrifice our dreams for our sons and daughters, a transformation takes place. We are free to accept a son or daughter in the present moment. Our dreams become grounded in God's dreams, which are richer and deeper than ours. Our vision can also be reshaped to appreciate God's timing, not ours. And through the grace of the Holy Spirit, we can watch for God's dreams, tucked away inside a daughter's or a son's wishes. Catherine gives us an example.

My dream is that my children come back to church. Like so many parents, my adult children no longer attend on a regular basis, and so I pray. I know that the seeds were planted in them and that these seeds will come to fruition in God's own time. But I did get excited last week when my daughter, who is an event planner, called to say that she is volunteering to help the local Catholic parish plan a big event. She thinks it is a networking opportunity for her professional life, but

I know that God is providing a networking opportunity for her spiritual life. I don't say that to her. That thought is just between me and God.

St. Elizabeth Seton (1774–1821) provides another example in sacrificing her own dreams for her son and seeking out God's dreams for him. William was a sailor in Massachusetts. At one point, he received a midshipman's order to report for a voyage on the *Independence*. The voyage meant separation and possible danger. So she put her map of Boston away and wrote a letter to her friend.

> This world of separations must have its course, and we must take its good and evil quietly as it passes. For my part, I am so accustomed to look only to our God in all that happens that it seems to me the most painful things increase our confidence and peace in Him, since all will draw us nearer to Himself, if only we kiss His hand as that of the best of Fathers.[6]

God's Dreams within a Grown Child's Dream

We can recognize and pray for God's dreams for a son or daughter within their own dreams. Therese remembers an experience of listening for God's dreams when our then-teenaged son Charlie wanted a unicycle for his birthday. Because of financial constraints, it was going to be a difficult request to honor. But Therese recognized how important this dream was because it was tied up with Charlie's participation in a clown-ministry group that visited hospitals and nursing homes. So Therese prayed, "You know what he really needs, Lord. So show me what to do, and I'll do it." The next morning, Therese was inspired to go to her first yard sale in over a year. And there it was, leaning against a garage door, right beside a box of tools: one unicycle in perfect condition. Of course, Charlie's dreams have changed many times since then, but she still tries to listen to all of them and to affirm his God-given dreams. Therese might even joke with God about a particular dream and ask, "Is this another unicycle, Jesus?"

The Advent-Christmas season and birthdays are good opportunities to enter this process of surrendering a son's or daughter's greatest desires as well as our own. It is a time to "go shopping," to ask God for a new awareness of a young person's spiritual, emotional, and intellectual dreams that often lie behind a birthday or Christmas desire. It is a time to weigh all our child's dreams, whether they are for material things, property, work, or peace of mind, in the light of God's love. So surrender all these desires, and watch for the gifts that only God can give. If we persist in surrendering our own intense desires to give good things to our children, God will give us a new glimpse of his hope and we will grow in our acceptance of his love.

If you then, who are evil, know how to give good gifts to your children, how much more will the heavenly Father give the Holy Spirit to those who ask him! (Luke 11:13)

Consecrate Our Relationships

Another step for entering into God's dreams for our daughters and sons is to consecrate our relationships with them and to offer God the bond between us. This kind of prayer blesses our children in a thousand different ways. It becomes a tiny mirror of the Father's surrender of his only Son, Jesus. When we give God the gift of our unfolding relationships, we unleash the love of God that is meant to flow between us, like a refreshing spring water in a quiet forest. The Holy Spirit, who orchestrates all prayer, will transform, mold, and restructure the parent-child relationship in new ways that reflect God's kingdom. Our children become our brothers and sisters in Jesus, which is part of God's greatest dream.

At this point, we want to share Vicky's witness about hopeful acceptance. Her story encompasses three years of prayerful surrender of her own dreams about her daughter's future. Vicky's experience teaches us that hopeful acceptance of God's loving concern is often the fruit of many hours of honest negotiations with God, as well as the constant reshaping of heart, mind, and soul.

When Vicky's daughter, Felicia, was in the middle of her first pregnancy, she left her husband, Roy, and asked to stay with her parents until she could get her life in order. Vicky said yes, hoping to encourage the couple to get counseling and reconcile. But in just a few short weeks, Felicia discovered that she had inoperable cancer. This was more than any of them could handle. Vicky was inconsolable. So she began to pray daily, begging God to spare her daughter and her grandchild from this life-threatening illness. And God was good. Paul was born without any complications, but Felicia was weak and didn't have the energy for counseling yet. So she stayed. Then Vicky prayed for the strength to take care of her grandson, since her husband worked fifty hours a week. God answered by sending Vicky's retired father into their home so that he could help with the baby. Grandpa provided child care during months of doctor's appointments. He read stories to Paul and even taught him how to count as he crawled up the stairs. Vicky was grateful.

But still, Felicia's cancer only got worse. Once again, Vicky prayed for her daughter's recovery and surrendered her to God. But Felicia only got sicker, and when her son was eighteen months old, she died. To make matters worse, her death was followed by the death of Vicky's dad. Vicky struggled with overwhelming feelings of loss and anger toward God. There had been no more healing, no time for marriage counseling, and no provisions made for legal custody of Paul. What could she do?

Sometimes God Has Another Plan

What happened next revolved around Felicia's husband, Roy, and his complicated response to his estranged wife's death. Roy became more and more resentful as he watched his in-laws raise the boy. On the day of his son's third birthday party, Roy stood up and said, "I'm taking my son home for good." And that is exactly what he did.

Vicky turned to her pastor. Fr. Tom advised her to pray a daily Rosary for Roy's conversion and to think about the situation for a while. As Vicky prayed, several things happened. First, God gave her compassion for Roy in his desire to be a good father.

Second, God challenged her to treat Roy as her own son. Vicky realized that she could have done more to affirm him. And as she was honest with herself, she realized that she really did not have the strength or energy to take care of Paul. So Vicky called Roy and apologized for specific actions. But she also insisted on visiting Paul for the sake of continuity in the child's life. Roy asked for two weeks before the first visit, then three more weeks, then another two months.

Vicky prayed for the grace to honor Roy's wishes, but her need to see Paul and her grandson's needs were also important. So she and her husband prayerfully decided to bring Roy to court for visitation rights and to let go of a custody claim. When the hearing came, the judge ruled in favor of a three-hour visit every two weeks. Many years have passed since then, and all of them, including Roy's new wife and their three additional children, enjoy being a family together. Vicky and her husband are now permitted to visit as often as they are able. Vicky's hopeful but firm acceptance of God's love for her daughter, her grandson, her son-in-law, and herself became a source of strength and healing for all of them.

What then are we to say about these things? If God is for us, who is against us? He . . . did not withhold his own Son, but gave him up for all of us. . . . Who will separate us from the love of Christ? Will hardship, or distress, or persecution, or famine, or nakedness, or peril, or sword? . . . No, in all these things we are more than conquerors through him who loved us. For I am convinced that neither death, nor life, nor angels, nor rulers, not things present, nor things to come . . . nor anything else in all creation, will be able to separate us from the love of God in Christ Jesus our Lord. (Romans 8:31-32, 35, 37-39)

God Is Love and Joy

Vicky's long-term struggles are not uncommon. Maybe your family has faced tragedies that leave you without hope. Perhaps even the idea of sorting out everyone's dreams and needs seems overwhelming. Ask Jesus your Savior for help. You are not alone. Recall those who sought Jesus in the Scriptures, like the men who lowered their friend through the roof into the house in which Jesus was speaking (Mark 2:1-12), or the woman suffering from a twelve-year hemorrhage who was healed by touching the hem of Jesus' cloak (Luke 8:43-48). Remember St. Elizabeth Seton, who prayed at her writing desk for her son, William, and then wrote, "Remember my favorite Xavier's prayer when you are in the raging tempest, 'Compassionate Lover of souls, save me.'"[7] Think about St. Thomas More (1478–1535), who wrote to his daughter, Margaret, to console her from his prison cell. He encouraged her to imagine her father sitting on God's lap, enjoying a little game that he had played with her as a child.

Psalm 37:4 also challenges us to lift up our dreams to God: "Take delight in the LORD, / and he will give you the desires of your heart." This advice translates into surrendering each and every desire for the sake of choosing Jesus as our greatest desire and as the source of all joy and goodness. Choosing Jesus enables us to rejoice no matter what the results of our prayers for our children. We can rejoice because we know the One who is the fulfillment of their biggest dreams. Jesus will draw them to himself. All that remains is to put our treasure hunt for smaller dreams into perspective. God will either grant the desires that unite us to Jesus or help us let go of the dreams that are obstacles to entering into the glory of God. There is always hope, whether it happens to us at the foot of the cross or while we delight in the empty tomb. Here is a sample prayer for choosing the gift of hope.

Jesus, I put aside what I want for my grown child. Come into my child's life and move him, ever so slightly, toward . . . [*a new job, a good spouse*] and toward your answer. If this dream will bring him closer to you, then let it happen. If it will not, then I choose your love, your ways, and your peace on his behalf. Show me the most important dreams underneath all of this so that my prayers will lie closer to your heart's desire for my son. I surrender myself into your capable hands. You are my hope. Amen.

Hope through the Eucharist

The call to live out the gift of hope is not something that we can do alone, at least not for very long. In addition to our private surrender prayers for our adult children, we encourage you to bring their needs to Jesus in the Eucharist. There are at least three distinct times in the celebration of the Eucharist when you can lift up your children to God. The first is during the Prayer of the Faithful, when you can silently lift up a child's needs along with the parish faith community: "For Ann, to be freed from her fear of ballooning mortgage payments, we pray to the Lord. For

Phil, who is worried that his new boss might eliminate his job, we pray to the Lord. For Michele, that she and her mother will be reconciled, we pray to the Lord. Lord, hear our prayer!"

Second, at the Offertory Prayer, you can lay all your cares and concerns for your grown children on the altar with the bread and wine. Ask Jesus to transform your heart so that you might have the strength of the Holy Spirit and a new compassion for your children. "Lord, I offer you my daughter Carrie, who is caught in the undertow of alcoholism and drug abuse. Into your hands, Father, I place my nephew Jeff, who lost his job again. Holy Spirit, I lift up my grandson Robbie, who is being treated for leukemia."

Third, when you receive the Eucharist, envision yourself carrying a particular adult child toward Jesus as you receive his Body and Blood. For many years, John imagined being one of the paralytic's friends who lowered the man into the house from the roof so that Jesus could heal him (Mark 2:1-12). On his way to Communion, John would choose one person to carry with him. "Lord Jesus, today I bring Stephen's girlfriend before you. She feels worthless because she cannot control her eating and lose weight" or "Lord Jesus, remove the burden of guilt that Charlie feels for his car accident" or "My Lord and my God, may Rose experience relief from the pain in her herniated disk." To pray this way is to move toward hopeful acceptance and even joy in God's transforming presence.

Rejoice in the Lord always; again I will say, Rejoice. Let your gentleness be known to everyone. The Lord is near. Do not worry about anything, but in everything by prayer and supplication with thanksgiving let your requests be made known to God. And the peace of God, which surpasses all understanding, will guard your hearts and your minds in Christ Jesus. (Philippians 4:4-7)

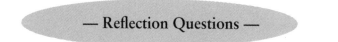

— Reflection Questions —

1. In what ways do you give voice to your hopes and dreams for your children? What does it mean to have hope in God and to rejoice in the Lord?

2. Make a list of *your* hopes and dreams for your sons and daughters. Examine each item and ask these questions: What does this dream say about me? About my child? How does this dream help or hinder my relationship with my son or daughter? How do I imagine God fulfilling this dream? What do I need to surrender to God? How might this happen?

3. Make a list of your son's or daughter's dreams. What is your response to one of these dreams? What feelings or thoughts do you experience when he or she mentions this dream? What patterns are in place that might prevent you from responding in love? How could you be more affirming about the positive elements of this desire?

—Prayer Skill—
Prayer for Healing of Memories

We can get stuck replaying a certain traumatic or an unpleasant event involving one of our children. Our minds keep coming back to this unpleasant memory. We get scared, so we push it away; but it keeps reappearing, and we see no way of escaping it. These memories can interfere with moving forward in faith. They can become like an unspoken theme song in our relationships with our loved ones. However, we can ask God to heal these memories in prayer by asking Jesus to come into the very situation that is troubling us.

Step One: Open your prayer by asking the Holy Spirit for guidance and healing. Then close your eyes and imagine an unpleasant event in a grown child's life. Perhaps it was a car accident, an illness, or an argument. Remember as many details as you can. Allow yourself to experience all the emotions.

Step Two: Imagine Jesus walking into the scene. You can pray, "Thank you for coming, Jesus. Help us now. Place your hand on my child, Jesus." Then focus on his face while you pray the name of Jesus until you can see Jesus approaching your loved one. Imagine Jesus doing whatever it takes to resolve the greatest needs.

Step Three: Thank God for what you have seen. Sing a hymn or pray Psalm 23.

CHAPTER FOUR

PRAYING FOR FORGIVENESS

O my God, forgive what I have been, correct what I am,
and direct what I shall be.

—St. Elizabeth Ann Seton

Therese's mom, Claire, taught us how important it is to offer and receive forgiveness. When Therese was four months pregnant with our third child, her mother had surgery for ulcerative colitis. Mom did not do well and required a second operation. It was just before this second operation that Therese and her mother had a very important conversation.

At first they shared news about Mom's coming grandchild and then about all the get-well cards that she had received. Finally, Mom took Therese's hand and said, "Please forgive me for anything and everything I ever did to hurt you, Therese." Therese responded with the same request. Later in the conversation, Claire interrupted her daughter to say, "I love you, Therese." She did this so often during their visit that Therese became embarrassed and told her so. Mom's reply was "You'll need to know." And she was right. Mom died two weeks later, but her message did not. She is still an important example of God's abiding love and mercy for each one of us.

Praying for forgiveness begins first with an honest look at family patterns in order to address bad behavior, human failings, and sinful choices. Next is the realization that we cannot forgive adequately by our own power. So we seek Jesus, who has overcome sin and has broken down all the obstacles between us. Finally, through prayer we enter into God's merciful love for others. Jesus enables us to forgive and be whole. Through prayer the effects of the life, death, and resurrection of Jesus are made manifest in our midst.

> But now in Christ Jesus you who once were far off have been brought near by the blood of Christ. For he is our peace; in his flesh he has made both groups into one and has broken down the dividing wall, that is, the hostility between us. (Ephesians 2:13-14)

In this chapter, we will consider ways that we can surrender our sinful and harmful behaviors toward family members as well as the immoral or hurtful actions of our adult sons and daughters. Then we will review ways to enter into God's mercy by examining the needs behind these failings. Finally, we will outline the process of seeking forgiveness, surrendering our actions, making reparation, and mending fractured relationships.

Repentance Brings Transformation

> Interior repentance is a radical reorientation of our whole life, a return, a conversion to God with all our heart, an end of sin, a turning away from evil. . . . It entails the desire and resolution to change one's life, with hope in God's mercy and trust in the help of his grace. (CCC 1431)

Praying for forgiveness means choosing to approach Jesus when he seems to be the farthest from us. It means seeking the strength to lift up personal stumbling blocks to love, along with the emotional, moral, and spiritual baggage that has led to sin. Surrendering these things allows us to step out of our broken lives and into the light. Prayer for forgiveness becomes a stepping-stone to freedom in Jesus Christ, who is Savior, Redeemer, and Prince of Peace. "The LORD is gracious and merciful, / slow to anger and abounding in steadfast love. / The LORD is good to all, / and his compassion is over all that he has made" (Psalm 145:8-9).

Praying for forgiveness is not about focusing on what we have done or what has been done to us. It is about lifting up the actions and omissions in our parent-child relationships to a merciful God. It is about giving Jesus all of our broken relationships, our inner struggles, our guilt, our sins, and our harmful actions. It is about approaching the Father in the name of his Son, Jesus, who has defeated sin. It is about discovering and rediscovering God's particular and unique compassion for each of our family members, especially when we fail to love one another.

When we pray for God's mercy, we can take our cue from the Apostles' Creed and the Nicene Creed, in which we confess belief in the forgiveness of sins. We can also seek the forgiveness that is part of the never-ending grace of the Sacraments of Baptism and Reconciliation. Through these sacraments, God gives us a new start in loving our families. Through the sacraments, we give flesh to our faith and trust Jesus with our failings. And even if our faith in God's gift of forgiveness is small, we move forward in faith by praying, "Lord I believe you forgive. Help my unbelief. Help me trust you with our actions toward each other." So let's take a closer look at what it means to receive the forgiveness of Jesus in prayer, especially as a believing parent. Let's consider the following prayers we can utter in God's presence as we seek God's forgiveness. They are (1) "Please forgive me"; (2) "Help me forgive myself"; (3) "Help me forgive my sons and daughters"; and (4) "Guide me into a merciful life."

"Please Forgive Me"

Lord Jesus Christ, Son of the living God,
have mercy on me, a sinner.

The simple Jesus Prayer is a good starting point for seeking forgiveness as a parent. It helps us take responsibility for our actions as mothers and fathers. We admit that our fallen human nature has colored our parenting and our day-to-day behaviors. We admit that we are not perfect parents. We conclude with St. Paul that "all have sinned and fall short of the glory of God" (Romans 3:23). We can examine the sins or wrongdoing that have disrupted our lives as the parents of children, teens, and young adults. We can examine occasions when we lacked affection, ignored primary needs, or rejected a child instead of just that child's bad behavior. Then we can surrender sinful behaviors and their effects on our relationships with our grown children.

The Jesus Prayer also focuses on Jesus as our redeemer and helps us avoid being centered on ourselves, our emotions, and what we feel we are entitled to. Jesus, our mediator, can show us our Father, the best of all parents. Jesus can help us to choose the Father's vision for us as parents. Finally, Jesus can release the power of his Holy Spirit in us, changing what needs to be changed. Jesus can send us the Spirit to remove the effects of our transgressions and help us move forward as parents of adult sons and daughters. Through Jesus we can become holy fathers and mothers, which is what is most essential in being instruments of God's mercy.

When praying for forgiveness, some parents list particular occasions of wrongdoing that still need God's merciful touch. Others pay attention to the failures of their present lives that trigger memories of wrongdoing from earlier decades. In either case, praying for forgiveness about a particular action also involves reviewing that action in its context. What happened before, during, and after the event? When you recall the details, picture Jesus in the midst of this particular memory. What would Jesus do to repair each person?

Keep in mind that an important goal in prayer is coming to terms with how you have loved and how you have failed to love. As you review your parenting life, take advantage of retreats, journaling, frequent celebration of the Sacrament of Reconciliation, and writing your life story. All are very appropriate, as is admitting your failures to your grown children and asking for their forgiveness. Remember, in the end, you must decide on a "theme song" for your life. Is it God's unending mercy, or is it bitterness and resentment?

"Help Me Forgive Myself"

Denise walked into John's office with a sad and heavy heart. She sat down with a sigh and shared that her daughter had just filed for divorce. But there was something more to her sadness. "It's all my fault," she added through a rush of tears. "If I had been able to make my marriage work, if I had not divorced her father, this would not be happening."

Almost every priest and counselor can tell you stories about parents who blame themselves for their grown children's failings. This kind of thinking does not help anyone; it is a dead end. Instead, we must visit and revisit forgiving ourselves in the name of Jesus for all real and perceived failings. We must pray, "Lord, have mercy, and bring me deeper into your endless love for me. I cannot love myself without you. I can't even truly know myself without looking through your eyes. Shower me with your unending mercy once again. I choose to forgive myself for your sake and for the sake of my family."

After you pray in this way, recall some very important spiritual principles. First, forgiving oneself is the product of a healthy daily relationship with God. It is based on a decision to enter and reenter the profound compassion of Jesus in prayer. Second, forgiveness of self should usher you into a genuine interest in the gift of discernment and measuring your actions and attitudes against the yardstick of the gospel. Third, forgiveness is the fruit of a daily examination of conscience—a sorting of sins, moments of weakness, and faulty attitudes. Self-examination helps us take responsibility for our actions and let go of responsibility for our children's problems and actions. Fourth, prayer for self-forgiveness is effective only if we make amends for actual sins and take steps to care for underlying needs. We might join a small support group, seek spiritual direction, or pursue healing through professional counseling.

Let's look at Denise's example through the lens of self-forgiveness. Yes, she probably did sin against her ex-husband. And he sinned against her as well, despite contributing circumstances such as lack of support, employment difficulties, and communication deficiencies that were no one's fault. And yes, damage was done to her daughter. But that is where Denise's responsibility ends. No one is responsible for another's actions. Her daughter's impending divorce is her daughter and son-in-law's responsibility, despite possible influences like a growing cultural breakdown in marriage, rampant misunderstanding about the Sacrament of Marriage, and employment patterns that hinder family life. So Denise cannot take primary responsibility for her daughter's divorce. Denise must ask Jesus to help her separate true moral guilt from regrets and human weaknesses that need healing. As one author points out, we need to trust in Jesus to do what seems impossible to us:

You have asked for forgiveness and can't repair the damage. Entrust it to the Lord. As we wait upon him, he can weave the darkened strands of sin into a beautiful tapestry, using it all for good in the final analysis. We have to trust him with that, because to repair sin's damage is often beyond our ability. Jesus, however, faces no impossible situations. He can do anything.[8]

"Help Me Forgive My Sons and Daughters"

Life presents us with many opportunities to forgive our grown sons and daughters. Maybe a son does not show up for Thanksgiving dinner. Perhaps a daughter has stolen Grandmother's jewelry from the attic. Maybe a grown child is abusing a spouse or a grandchild. These actions, of course, have varying degrees of severity and a wide range of consequences in our families. Facing any of these actions or any kind of sin in prayer is not easy. It helps to contemplate the mercy and forgiveness of Jesus that is evident in countless scriptural healing stories. In Mark 2:1-12, for example, Jesus not only forgives a paralytic man, but he also heals him. He teaches us how intimately the two are woven together. We can also contemplate Jesus on the cross. Despite his excruciating pain and the injustice committed against him, he chooses to forgive the nearby thief and all those who put him to death. So imitate Jesus by choosing to become an instrument of forgiveness and healing, both in prayer and in the parent-adult child relationship.

Therese's dad stands out as an example of someone who pursued forgiveness. When one of his daughters had a child with a black partner, Dad prayed for the power to forgive her and the strength to let go of his own racial prejudice. Over time, God helped him love his new little granddaughter and get beyond his feelings. Then God led him to take yet another step. About a year after his granddaughter's birth, he visited his sister's daughter, Peggy, who had married a black man fifteen years earlier. "Please forgive me for not loving you and your husband the way I should have," he told her. "I don't want to be like that anymore." That conversation was one of the first things that Peggy told us about when we met at a family reunion years later. "I'll never forget it. That took a lot of love," she said.

Corrie ten Boom is another example. A Dutch Christian, she was a prisoner in a World War II concentration camp because she and her family were caught hiding Jews in their home. Several years after Corrie's release, following a talk that she had given on forgiveness, a German prison guard from the same camp approached her. "I am so glad you forgive me," he said. She was shocked. Did she? Corrie was challenged by her own words, but by the grace of God, she was able to extend her hand in friendship to the man. "Forgiveness is an act of the will," she wrote, "and the will can function regardless of the temperature of the heart."[9]

Therese recalls another example from her life. She was complaining to God about the lack of phone calls from one of our daughters. Then God reminded her of her own reluctance to call her brother, who was suffering from stage-four liver cancer. It was difficult to do, even though she had promised to make weekly phone calls after his initial diagnosis. God's reminder gave her new compassion and forgiveness for our daughter. Praying also brought to mind important steps for forgiving others, especially family members who have seen us at our best and our worst.

How do we go about forgiving our sons and daughters? First, decide to forgive, and ask for the gifts of compassion, forgiveness, and understanding. Second, let go of your underlying needs and the things you feel you were entitled to and didn't get. Third, look at a son's or daughter's behavior as if it were your own. Ask Jesus how you have wronged someone else in the same way. Praying for the grace to see one's own failings is an important step in appreciating God's compassion for family members. Fourth, choose an act of kindness toward this person. We are called to live as witnesses to the redeeming love of Christ, which draws us ever closer to one another.

"Guide Me into a Merciful Life"

O come, let us worship and bow down,
   let us kneel before the LORD, our Maker!
For he is our God,
   and we are the people of his pasture,
   and the sheep of his hand.
O that today you would listen to his voice!
   Do not harden your hearts. (Psalm 95:6-8)

John's most meaningful experience of family forgiveness revolves around his grandfather, Joseph, who owned a brickyard on Plantation Street in Worcester, Massachusetts, from about 1890 to 1915. As the story goes, he was a hard-hearted man who managed many rough-and-tumble workers. Unfortunately, he was also hard on his oldest daughter, Emily, when she married against his wishes. In his will, Joseph not only disowned Emily, but after her untimely death, he sent most of her children to an orphanage. For many months after the discovery of his grandfather's actions and his will, it was difficult for John to teach about forgiveness. He tried praying with a brick from the Plantation Street brickyard but still could not forgive Joseph. Instead, John felt even more ashamed about having Joseph as his middle name, after his grandfather.

Then God used a series of events to help John. First, John began to make visits to the brickyard and Therese began to research its history. John could see the good work that had been done there. Second, Therese published a comprehensive article about the brickyard online. A few months later, one of Emily's estranged great-granddaughters, Carol, saw the article and contacted

Therese. We were amazed. Finally, when John's brother died, we drove home for the wake and funeral. Carol came to the wake and greeted Therese, who brought her to John. After a somber introduction, John put his arms around Carol and asked her forgiveness on behalf of his grandfather. It was a healing moment for both of them. What had been severed was made whole. What had been broken was redeemed and healed. The grace of God's mercy prevailed at this little family reunion.

> In him we have redemption through his blood, the forgiveness of our trespasses, according to the riches of his grace that he lavished on us. With all wisdom and insight he has made known to us the mystery of his will . . . to gather up all things in him, things in heaven and things on earth. (Ephesians 1:7-10)

In most instances, it is not easy to forgive ourselves, our grown children, or other important members of our families. But it is an integral part of choosing God's love as the center of family life. And even though it may not be a vision that you share with a spouse or grown sons and daughters, God will honor your choice to forgive and your prayers. We must trust the results of our forgiveness prayers to God as we watch for his intervention, his healing, and his mending of what has been torn apart. The Holy Spirit will be unleashed in new ways. Jesus will usher you through many conversions of mind, heart, and soul in the wake of your decision. God is faithful and removes our sins from us.

We end with another example of family-wide forgiveness and healing. It was Richard's seventy-fifth birthday and a very sad day as well. His grandson, Matt, had been arrested for drug possession. "What should I say to Matt's parents and to all my distraught children?" he wondered that morning. Then God gave him an answer. When his birthday party was well underway and his daughter stood up to get the birthday cake, he stopped her. "Just a minute!" he interrupted as he fetched an oversized bag from under his chair. "We have to take care of Matt first." Everyone waited. Then he produced a statue of Mary and a handful of rosary beads. "It's time for us to pray for Matt." It seems that they had prayed together as a young family. And now it was just what they needed in order to forgive this young boy. Despite the tears, they all reached out to God with one voice and surrendered their pain. And God gave them renewed strength as they prayed and cried together.

Authentic knowledge of the God of mercy, the God of tender love, is a constant and inexhaustible source of conversion, not only as a momentary interior act but also as a permanent attitude, as a state of mind. Those who come to know God in this way, who "see" Him in this way, can live only in a state of being continually converted to Him. . . . This state of conversion . . . marks out the most profound element of the pilgrimage of every man and woman on earth.

—Blessed John Paul II[10]

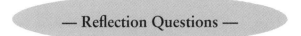
— Reflection Questions —

1. What is your understanding of the ways in which Jesus forgave people in the New Testament? Which example inspires you? What comes to mind when you think about asking Jesus for forgiveness and mercy in prayer?

2. What is it like for you to forgive yourself? How does this experience differ from the act of forgiving others? What would it take for you to embrace God's mercy toward yourself and your family in a more meaningful way?

3. What are some of the patterns for addressing wrongdoing and sin in your family? How is reconciliation a part of your family life? What obstacles prevent this from happening? What strategies has your family used to overcome these obstacles?

—Prayer Skill—
The Rosary as a Tool of Reconciliation

Whether or not you usually pray the Rosary, you can use parts of the Rosary as you pray for your adult sons and daughters. We suggest two brief adaptations for seeking Mary's help. As our Mother, she will lead us into a greater awareness of God's mercy, healing, and forgiveness toward our families.

John's Rosary Walk: John used to be torn between walking and praying at lunchtime, but not anymore. Now he walks and prays a decade of the Rosary for each member of our family. First, he prays an Our Father for everybody at once. Then, he starts in birth order and prays for individual sons, daughters, a son-in-law, and grand-children. "Bless Ann," he says, and then he prays a Hail Mary while picturing her in his mind's eye. Next comes Charlie, then Claire and our son-in-law, Bruce, and then the other children. Sometimes he adds another Rosary for our "spiritual" children, like a niece who recently moved to Argentina. John says, "I guess I'm lucky we have only five children, one son-in-law, and four grandchildren. They fit nicely into two Rosaries. By the time we have more, I hope to be retired. I will need the extra time for more Hail Marys!"

Therese's Rosary Ingredients: Some time ago, when Therese was anxious about a serious family problem and couldn't get to sleep, she stumbled upon a way to use parts of the Rosary to pray for a grown son or daughter. The shortness of the prayer gave Therese more relief from her anxiety.

Step One: Choose a photo of this loved one (either a printed picture or one on your computer).

Step Two: Close your eyes and greet Mary through the entire Hail Mary prayer or through a song.

Step Three: Prayerfully repeat the second half of the Hail Mary for your grown child:

Holy Mary, mother of God and mother of _____
(*name*), pray for (*him/her*) now and at the hour of (*his/her*) death. Amen.

Spend as little as five minutes or as long as twenty minutes praying this abbreviated version of the prayer. When praying for a couple, add a second name (mother of *Gary and Beth*, pray for them).

Step Four: End with the following prayer from the Chaplet of Divine Mercy:

Eternal God, in whom mercy is endless and the treasury of compassion inexhaustible, look kindly upon us, and increase Your mercy in us, that in difficult moments we might not despair nor become despondent, but with great confidence submit ourselves to Your holy will, which is Love and Mercy itself. Amen.

CHAPTER FIVE

PRAYING FOR PATIENT TRUST

Let nothing disturb you,
let nothing frighten you,
all things are passing;
Patient endurance attains all things:
One who God possesses wants nothing,
for God alone suffices.
—St. Teresa of Ávila (1515–1582)

When Therese's mother died, her grandmother's sister, Lillie, became Therese's second mother and a grandmother for our young children. She was well over eighty at the time. We visited her often in her tiny two-room apartment in an assisted living facility, where Aunt Lillie was pleased that she could be surrounded by her most precious belongings. Two antique pillows sat like bookends on her flowered couch, holding a place for visitors. Her brass teakettle sat perched on the stove, ready to provide refreshment at a moment's notice. But during one visit, we noticed a curious item on Aunt Lillie's reading table next to her rosary beads. It was a shot glass filled with coins. Therese asked, "What's the shot glass for?"

"Oh, that," she laughed, slowly fingering the clear crystal as if to unveil her latest treasure. "I found it among Aunt Hattie's things. And you know, it's just what I needed." She interrupted herself with a few soft giggles, emptying the glass into her wrinkled hand. "I don't want to forget anyone when I say my prayers at noontime. This penny means one Our Father, one Hail Mary, and one Glory Be for Carol. This penny is for Blanche across the hall. This one is for your grandmother. The nickels are for Rosaries. One is for Claire and one is for you. One is for Brenda—we haven't heard from her for almost eight months now. This way I won't forget anybody. You have to play tricks on yourself when you get to be my age."

Aunt Lillie was patient and faithful in prayer. She prayed for several hours each day until her death at one hundred. We try to imitate her by offering Jesus each of our grown children on a daily basis. But there is more to intercessory prayer than repetition, especially for someone like Aunt Lillie. At the heart of such prayer is a long-term commitment to enter into God's presence on behalf of a daughter or son. We approach God in a son's or daughter's name in an act of *sacrifice*, which literally means to "make (them) holy." We also act like a bridge, because they belong to us and to God at the same time. Sometimes we pray from a frazzled state of disbelief and anxiety, but still we lift them up to Jesus. Sometimes, when we feel unable to let go of our loved ones, Jesus embraces us and moves us (and our children) forward in the presence of his Father. Intercessory prayer is about connecting with God, whether our prayers are like a delicate thread or a sturdy wire cable. God's presence becomes a source of blessing and strength for us and for our sons and daughters, even if the results of our prayers are invisible.

Wait and Be Stretched

Some would say that waiting patiently is a lost art in our society. Who enjoys waiting in heavy traffic? Who welcomes a delay at the doctor's office, at a restaurant, or at the supermarket checkout? And if we add our Internet experiences to the mix, who waits patiently for a "slow" web page to open? Who remains calm when an e-mail response takes more than forty-eight hours? Our cultural experiences with waiting make it difficult for us to wait for God's response to our prayers. But if we look at it another way, letting God teach us how to wait may be just the antidote that we need to live as disciples of Jesus.

> The LORD is the everlasting God,
>   the Creator of the ends of the earth.
> He does not faint or grow weary, . . .
> He gives power to the faint,
>   and strengthens the powerless.
> Even youths will faint and be weary . . .
> but those who wait for the LORD shall renew their strength,
>   they shall mount up with wings like eagles,
> they shall run and not be weary,
>   they shall walk and not faint. (Isaiah 40:28-31)

Some of the saints show us how to "wait for the Lord," as described by the prophet Isaiah. St. Teresa of Ávila, for example, gave God every concern about her sisters, and then waited, undisturbed, for God's instructions. St. Monica (331–387), the long-suffering mother of St. Augustine, waited for God's response to her prayers about her son, even though it took decades. Sts. Joachim and Anne, the grandparents of Jesus, are said to have prayed for a child for twenty years until they finally conceived a baby girl named Mary. We, too, can surrender our anxieties and our tendency to dictate the timing of God's response. We, too, can surrender our emotions and choose to trust in the Lord at all times.

Expectant prayer is also like planting a tiny mustard seed. Our small seed of faith contains all the important ingredients—all the "spiritual DNA" necessary—to bring about God's kingdom in our families. Jesus reassures us about the power of our decision to pray. He promises that "nothing will be impossible for you" (Matthew 17:20). And so we persist in approaching Jesus until the seed turns into a seedling, then a budding plant, and then a full-grown flowering bush. We ask for the Holy Spirit to give us the gift of prayer over and over again. We ask the Spirit to help us avoid pounding the ground in frustration. We ask the Spirit to help us resist digging up an immature seedling or fight the urge to walk away from the task of tending the garden of family life. "I believe; help my unbelief!" (Mark 9:24). The act of praying for a loved one over a long period of time is in itself an act of faith. We expect that God can do something, or we wouldn't bother with prayer.

Wait for the Lord's Strength

Betty is an example of active waiting in prayer as she intercedes for her son-in-law, Ted. She knows what it means to dwell on the cutting edge of patient trust. Betty has turned to Jesus almost every day for six years asking him to heal her son-in-law. At each step in her journey, she has faced a new opportunity to intercede and to wait upon the Lord. Betty is keenly aware of the strength that flows from speaking with Jesus, who "is able for all time to save those who approach God through him, since he always lives to make intercession for them" (Hebrews 7:25). Here is what she writes:

I gave birth to each biological child once, but I have given birth to my son-in-law, Ted, a thousand times in prayer. Ted had a childhood filled with unimaginable horrors that ended in estrangement from his mother and now-deceased grandparents. Years later Ted realized that his grandparents were buried not too far from our home, although he didn't remember the name of the city. So I searched and found their grave and brought Ted and my daughter there. He approached their headstone slowly and said, "Grammy, Pop Pop, this is my wife, Connie." God had begun the healing in Ted.

So with his permission, I searched for the rest of Ted's family. Many months later, I located his mother, Claudia, by phone on Mother's Day. What a joy it was to share news about our mutual granddaughters and to mail her photos! But Ted was still unwilling to visit her. So I prayed and arranged for my own visit with Claudia, especially after discovering that she had stage-four cancer. When we greeted each other, Claudia said, "When I hug you, I feel like I'm hugging Ted." I replied, "And when I hug you, *I* feel like I'm hugging Ted!" She gave me a photo album of

Ted's childhood and small gifts for his children. It was an important connection for both of us.

But two more years passed, and still there was no reconciliation between Claudia and Ted, no visits, just a flood of raw memories for Ted and a downward medical spiral for Claudia. She died alone. And Ted could not even bring himself to attend her funeral. Instead, Ted's aunt placed Claudia's precious photos of his family in her casket. So now I pray that maybe he might visit her grave and be healed or that Jesus will tend his wounds in a way that glorifies the Father.

Surrender the Gift of Time

Constant intercessory prayer for a son or daughter takes time. So allow God to stretch and redefine your perceptions of time. First, surrender the gift of time by committing yourself to praying for your child on a regular basis. Step out of "clock" time and into the fullness of time. Step into that place where God's love is "the same yesterday and today and forever" (Hebrews 13:8). Second, pray with respect for the time it may take for a daughter or son to grow into adulthood, then into middle age and beyond. Give them the time and the room they need to figure things out for themselves. A humorous example involves our prayers for our son Stephen to overcome his apprehensions about water while working at the oceanfront. His solution was to check out a book from the library about swimming. After reading it, he would then thrash about in the water for a couple of hours. He did this until he felt comfortable and could swim. We wouldn't have done it that way, but it worked for him.

For everything there is a season, and a time for every matter under heaven:
a time to be born, and a time to die;
a time to plant, and a time to pluck up what is planted; . . .
a time to weep, and a time to laugh;
a time to mourn, and a time to dance; . . .
a time to embrace, and a time to refrain from embracing.
(Ecclesiastes 3:1-2, 4, 5)

A third step is to submit to God's sense of time, to God's pace
for answering us, whether it takes a month, a year, or even beyond
our lifetimes. Trust God. The waters of Baptism are a dynamic,
moving force in the lives of your grown sons and daughters.
Something *is* happening! So guard against stagnant, wooden, and
unemotional prayers. Guard against a frozen faith that leaves you
paralyzed. Climb the bone-chilling mountain of discarded hopes
and what seems like broken promises. Then surrender to God's
sense of timing. Let him teach you to view all things from the
perspective of eternity.

Negotiate with Jesus again and again. There are many ways
that the needs of your son or daughter might be met. Work
things out with God in prayer—verbally, in a written journal, through music and movement—whatever allows you to
speak and to listen with a heart that is open to direction. One
father finds himself praying in angry outbursts about what God
has not done. "It clears the air between us. I know God is big
enough to take it. And then I am free to ask for God's help," he
explains. Another parent, Elaine, shares this: "Knowing Jesus as
my Savior is the best thing that ever happened to me. I love my

kids and grandkids and great-grandkids very much, but there are some challenges at times that keep me storming the gates of heaven again and again. And I can say that every time I do, Jesus is faithful."

Putting Our Adult Children in God's Hands and Heart

Trust in the LORD, and do good. . . .
Take delight in the LORD,
  and he will give you the desires of your heart.
Commit your way to the LORD;
  trust in him, and he will act. (Psalm 37:3-5)

One woman, Mary Lou Quinlan, describes how her now-deceased mother exhibited her enduring commitment to trust in God by using a "God Box" to place her petitions. "Mom would scrounge up any old piece of paper—the back of a receipt, a torn paper towel, or a while-you-were-out slip sufficed—date it, and write, 'Dear God,' followed by her concern of the moment, which ran the gamut from big ('Please let our house sell today') to small ('Please let Mary Lou's Pergo floor be the right choice')." As Mary Lou observed, "The simple act of writing down the wish and relinquishing control to a higher power was her way to help others, and relieve her own mind."

Years later, when her mom died, Mary Lou was surprised to find ten God Boxes in her mom's closet. When she opened them, "we were face-to-face with every mountain and molehill we had ever confided to Mom. In the God Boxes, she had left a twenty-year love letter to us in hundreds of pieces." A few years later,

Mary Lou started her own God Box. She writes of this experience with her dying father:

Alone with Dad, . . . exhausted and desperate, I grabbed a piece of lined yellow paper and scrawled, "Dear God (and Mom), Dad has been so strong for so long. I know you don't want him to be in pain. I never thought I could ask this . . . but please bring Daddy to heaven, into your arms. Thank you, Always your girl, Mary Lou." I folded it small and put it in one of Mom's old God Boxes. I felt her calming hand on me. My heart finally lifted. And Dad died peacefully three days later.[11]

In God's Providence

We firmly believe that God is master of the world and of its history. But the ways of his providence are often unknown to us. Only at the end, when our partial knowledge ceases, when we see God "face to face," will we fully know the ways by which—even through the dramas of evil and sin— God has guided his creation to that definitive sabbath rest for which he created heaven and earth. (CCC 314)

Praying with patient trust is a way of handing our sons' and daughters' difficulties over to God's providential care. We give our loved ones to the Father in the same way that Jesus handed his life over to the Father in the Garden of Gethsemane (Luke 22:35-54). We can learn many things from the way Jesus did this. First, he cried out to his Father. He was honest; he admitted his pain and his needs. Then, he submitted to the Father's love. We, too, can surrender our sons and daughters to the Father, who loves them beyond all measure and provides for their every breath, even in the midst of hardship. It is true that this kind of trust does not come easily. It takes work. It requires us to let go, the way we did when we left our little one with a babysitter for the first time or walked away from our teenager's first dorm room. "Lord, I believe; help my unbelief!" (Mark 9:24).

Many years ago, Therese learned a lot about God's providential love. It happened when our daughter Rose was about three, during our "medical outpatient summer." In a few brief weeks, John had surgery on his ankle, Charlie had surgery on his knee, and Stephen had an infected toenail removed at the hospital. Needless to say, Therese had her hands full. During one very hectic day, little Rose volunteered to bring crackers to her incapacitated moaning brother, who was draped across our wooden rocking chair in the living room. In her zeal, Rose skidded around the corner and smashed her forehead on the rocking chair. She emerged with a very deep and bloody gash. Off we went to the emergency room for stitches.

After the wound was cleansed, the nurse put Rose in a papoose, and Therese followed them into the OR. For every moment of that procedure, Rose had her eyes glued on Therese's face—she did not look away once or even blink. Her mother's face was her redemption. What an awesome responsibility for Therese! She remembers praying, "Help me keep my inner eye glued to your face, Jesus. Help me to focus on you so that I can give this little person hope." We both remember this experience often as we pray for our children. "To you I lift up my eyes, . . . / as the eyes of a maid / to the hand of her mistress, / so our eyes look to the LORD our God, / until he has mercy upon us" (Psalm 123:1, 2).

Another example of surrendering to God's providential love involves Agostino and Stella Cabrini, parents of St. Frances Cabrini. Francesca was their tenth child, born two months prematurely, into a family that would bury seven of their young children. Over the years, Stella prayed about Francesca's delicate constitution, surrendering her to God often, especially after a near drowning at the age of seven that led to severe bronchitis, which lasted for several years. Later, her mother's concern would become the inspiration for St. Frances, who had a special love for children in need. On the last day of Frances' life, she insisted on helping pack five hundred boxes of candy for immigrant children.

Trust in the Lord at All Times

At this point, we would like to share some examples of patient trust in prayer. These people remind us that patient trust is not something we do. It is a gift that is given to us by God just when we need it most. It encompasses being committed, leaning on God, drawing strength from God, and taking refuge in Jesus. It can be as simple as praying with the rhythm of your breath: *inhale* (I accept your love); *exhale* (I surrender). It can be as profound as standing firm in the midst of a spiritual hurricane.

Edith Stein (1891–1942) had grown up in a Jewish family but was an atheist and a professor at a university when a colleague and friend died suddenly. She offered to help the colleague's wife pack up important books and papers. As Edith walked into her friend's home, she expected to find an overwrought, distressed widow. Instead, she met a woman of strength and trust. The woman's example was a powerful witness to Edith: "For the first time I was seeing with my very eyes the church, triumphant over the sting of death. That was the moment that my unbelief collapsed and Christ shone forth—in the mystery of the cross."[12] Edith would go on to become a Catholic, a contemplative nun, a holocaust victim during World War II, and a canonized saint, St. Teresa Benedicta of the Cross.

A friend named Margaret shares God's challenge to take refuge in prayer. This invitation first came from her experience in the confessional:

> "My son Jude is in trouble again! His wife wants a divorce," she blurted out.
> "You need to pray for him," Father replied.
> "But I pray for him every day, and things only get worse!"
> Father nodded and said, "Just keep praying anyway."
> "But it doesn't do any good!"
> "Keep praying."

Margaret's story mirrors the story of many parents who continue to pray despite the great distress they experience about situations in the lives of their adult sons and daughters . Margaret kept praying through her son's psychological, spiritual, and marital problems. When those problems became more than her son could handle, he committed suicide. Margaret was devastated, but she never gave up praying. Like St. Peter, she kept her eyes on Jesus, and she stayed above the turbulent water as long as she remained focused on him. And after burying her son's remains with his grandparents, instead of scattering them, as his friends had wished, she felt a new and growing peace.

Today Jesus continues to call out to every parent like Margaret who is desperately searching for hope. So move forward even when you are afraid of drowning in sorrow. Keep walking. Keep praying. Jesus will lift you up. Jesus will help you stand in the power of the Holy Spirit, who is the forerunner of peace.

[God,] in the shipwreck of this present life, sustain me by the plank of prayer, lest I sink by my own weight. Instead, let the hand of your mercy raise me up.

—St. Gregory the Great (540–604)

St. Jane de Chantal (1572–1641) was a wife and mother of four when her husband died in a hunting accident. Still, she remained generous, forgiving, and kind. She even became the godmother of the child of her husband's killer. Jane trusted God about her children's future when she founded a religious community. As disciples of Jesus who are also parents, we can be gently encouraged to trust in Jesus by praying her prayer:

O Lord Jesus, I surrender to you all my will. Let me be your lute. Touch any string you please. Always and forever let me make music in perfect harmony with your own. Yes, Lord, with no ifs, ands, or buts, let your will be done in this family, for the father, for the children, for everything that concerns us, and especially let your will be done in me.[13]

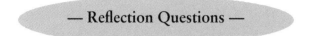

— Reflection Questions —

1. What is most frustrating about waiting in traffic or in a long line at the checkout counter? How is your experience of waiting in these situations the same or different from waiting for God to answer your prayers? What could you do to be more successful at waiting on the Lord?

2. How do you view time? Is it something that you spend? Is it something that escapes your grasp? Is it a precious gift or a puzzle to be solved? What does it mean to surrender your time to God in prayer?

3. What does it mean to abandon oneself to divine providence, to God's protection and care? Who has been a model for relying on God? When have you been able to let go of difficulties and trust God?

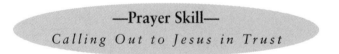

—Prayer Skill—

Calling Out to Jesus in Trust

"Rejoice that your names are written in heaven." (Luke 10:20)

During a Lenten outreach program in the Archdiocese of Boston, our friend David Thorp taught many people how to pray for their loved ones, especially for those who had stopped going to church. At the end of each presentation, David invited his listeners to write the name of a loved one in a small black book. He promised to carry this book in his jacket pocket and pray for these people every day. Then, just a few months later, David died. His grieving family placed the black book in his casket so that he could carry those names all the way to heaven. But after the funeral, it was retrieved by his co-workers so that they could continue to pray for all of his loved ones by name.

Step One: Opening prayer (by Blessed John Martin Moye, 1730–1793):

Providence of my God, I adore you in all your designs. I place my destiny [and my child's destiny] in your hands, confiding to you all that I have, all that I am, and all that I am to become.

Step Two: Make a list of your grown children and those whom you have spiritually adopted. At the bottom of the list, write, "I give each one to you, Jesus. And I ask your forgiveness for my sins against each one and against all of them." Then fold your list as a way of acknowledging that God's plan is often hidden from our eyes.

Step Three: Think about the hundreds of people who have called out to Jesus. Imagine yourself in such a crowd. Choose one or two of the following scriptural titles of Jesus. Then use them to call out to him in trust. While doing so, stretch out your hand and your list to Jesus. Reach out to him from the crowd. Spend as much or as little time as you need to give your sons or daughters to him. You might also intersperse these titles with "Touch my daughter (or son), _____ (*name*)."

Alpha and Omega | Anointed High Priest | Jesus
Beloved One | Bread of Life | Prince of Peace
Blessed One | Teacher | Morning Star
Christ | Chosen One | Christ the King | Lord
Emmanuel | Faithful One

Ω

Holy One of God | Good Shepherd | Healer
I AM | High Priest | Holy Servant | Just One
King of Israel | Master | King of Kings | Redeemer
Lamb of God | My King | Lion of Judah
Lord of Glory

Ω

Light of the World | Living Bread
Key of David | Man of Sorrows | Rabbi
Servant of God | Savior of the World | Savior
Shepherd | Son of David | Son of God
Suffering Servant | Son of Mary
Word of God | Truth and Life

Ω

Step Four: Thank God for hearing you by praying this psalm:

For God alone my soul waits in silence,
　　for my hope is from him.
He alone is my rock and my salvation,
　　my fortress; I shall not be shaken. (Psalm 62:5-6)

CHAPTER SIX

PRAYING FOR THE SPIRITUAL LIVES OF OUR ADULT CHILDREN

As a young adult in today's dynamic society, I—like so many other young adults—am hungry. I have felt a strong spiritual hunger, a hunger that stems from the need to discover who I am, who is my God, and what is my purpose in society. It is a hunger that once fed can continue to fuel my life journey in a direction that would follow the footsteps of Christ.
—Michelle M. Mystkowski, Patchogue, NewYork[14]

Michelle's statement marks the transition between the first and second sections of our book about lifting up our adult sons and daughters into God's presence. We chose Michelle's description of spiritual hunger for several reasons. First, Michelle is like most grown children who speak about "spiritual" rather than "religious" needs. Second, Michelle encourages us to focus on young people's experiences as a starting point for prayer. Third, as parents, we are familiar with a son's or daughter's hungers. We fed them as children, whether they were physically hungry or hungry for attention. We either went to the refrigerator, or we offered them a hug and a few moments of our time. But now their hungers are more complex. So we often ask ourselves, "What is spiritual hunger? Why don't they just bring their spiritual needs to church? Why don't they go to Mass? Where did I go wrong?"

If these are your questions, then you are not alone. More than 80 percent of the young adults who were raised as Catholics are inactive in their faith.[15] Some experience a prolonged search for spiritual identity and confusion about where to turn for the answers to life's important questions. Some are simply disinterested in God and/or the Church. Some see organized religion as irrelevant and impersonal. Some feel like unwelcomed "strangers in the house of God."[16] Their conclusions and distinctions between "spiritual" and "religious" may seem foreign to us, so let's first take a closer look at the idea of spiritual hunger. And let's consider a bouquet of spiritual needs that present young people (and some parents) with new opportunities for reaching out to God.

In Search of Meaning

Our times are both momentous and fascinating. While on the one hand people seem to be pursuing material prosperity and to be sinking ever deeper into consumerism and materialism, on the other hand we are witnessing a desperate search for meaning, the need for an inner life, and a desire to learn new forms and methods of meditation and prayer.

—Blessed John Paul II[17]

The young adult's search for meaning underscores an important reality about the human person: every one of us searches for perfect love, for the ultimate meaning of life, and for clues about our final destiny. This is the way the human person is hardwired by God—parents and children alike. What may be different is that we, as parents, are older and have had more experience with life. We have learned that some things that seem to promise happiness, such as wealth, honor, or prestige, are dead ends—they don't lead to true or long-lasting happiness. In addition, because of the times in which we grew up, we may have struggled with an ongoing call to a relationship with God only within the context of several generations of parish family life. We simply don't see how the two could be separated.

O LORD, you have searched me and known me.
You know when I sit down and when I rise up. . . .
If I take the wings of the morning
    and settle at the farthest limits of the sea,
even there your hand shall lead me,
    and your right hand shall hold me fast.
(Psalm 139:1-2, 9-10)

So part of our call as parents is to nurture a young person's search for meaning on their own terms and as individuals searching for God's presence. We can begin by meditating on times of childhood happiness and turning points in their lives, such as a graduation from college or the death of a grandparent. Every significant life event has already shaped them and awakened spiritual longings. Are you familiar with how these experiences have molded your grown child? Have you meditated on their meaning? Have you ever talked with that child about his journey from childish to adult definitions of love or truth? Do you have a realistic picture of that child's inner life? And if you have several children, how have you prayed for their spiritual lives on an individual basis?

One strategy for nurturing your children is to pray about their deepest desires in spiritual terms. For example, one young person in our family wants to be rich. So we often ask God to pour out his spiritual wealth and riches on this young man. We pray with Scripture passages such as Ephesians 1:17-19 about our inheritance in Jesus.

As parents, we can also collect the prayers we have for our children and the Scripture passages that we pray into a small notebook or diary—one for each grown child—and add to it often. We might also add any spiritual experiences that a son or daughter has shared with us. Here is one such experience that could be recorded in a parent's diary.

> Jennifer had been going to Alanon meetings for quite some time. Often when it came to the part about surrendering to a higher power, she felt uncomfortable. Somehow her New Age gods did not seem to be adequate any longer. So she found herself consciously talking to Jesus again for the first time in many years. And I am so glad that she felt free enough to share this with me as we spoke about our experiences of praying for her ex-husband and daughter.

Ask for the Gift of Faith

When you pray about the spiritual hungers of your children, you are entering into a paradox. On the one hand, you are asking for a gift that seems absent, especially if your son or daughter is not a regular churchgoer. But on the other hand, you are seeking what has already been given to that child in Baptism. So revisit what that baptismal faith means, especially if your grown children have chosen New Age beliefs. Review your own faith by praying one of the Creeds. Start by affirming your faith in God the Father, "Creator of heaven and earth." Then ask God to continue creating your son or daughter. Pray to Jesus who is "true God" and "Light from Light." Then ask the Holy Spirit to draw you and your child into the communion of saints in whatever way is best. Finally, step back and surrender all your own spiritual hungers to God, realizing your total dependence on the grace of Baptism, the grace that you sought at your son's or daughter's Baptism.

As parents, we can also become more aware of the different types of spiritual hungers that are really opportunities for new faith.[18] Then our awareness of which one is taking center stage in a daughter's or son's life becomes another good starting point for prayer. (Also, keep in mind that these hungers do not arise in any particular order.)

- The hunger for the source of all life underlies a call to *spiritual conversion*. Blessed Kateri Tekakwitha (1656–1680) discovered a personal God through the Jesuit missionaries. She was able to redefine life as a sacred gift from the Father.

- The hunger for a perfect best friend who is bigger than pain and death underlies a call to *Christian conversion*. St. Francis of Assisi (1181–1226) gave himself in unconditional self-surrender to Jesus.

- The hunger for a supportive, forgiving spiritual community underlies a call to a vital universal faith community. St. Elizabeth Seton experienced this kind of *ecclesial conversion* through compassionate Catholic friends in Italy.

- The hunger for a truth that stands up to any and all questions underlies a call to intellectual conversion. Blessed Carlos Rodriguez (1918–1963) from Puerto Rico helped many young people experience this kind of conversion by teaching them about God.

- The hunger for fairness and personal integrity underlies the call to moral conversion. It means choosing God as the reference point for all actions, as St. Augustine did.

- The desire to make a difference and transform the world is at the heart of sociopolitical conversion. St. Martin de Porres (1579–1639) fed and cared for hundreds of poor people in Lima, Peru, and established an orphanage for abandoned children.

Hunger for a Spiritual Home

One of the spiritual hungers that concerns many parents is the hunger for a faith community. We want our grown children to know the strength that we have found in the arms of the Church. We want them to come home and sit beside us on Sundays. We want Jesus to open the church doors for their return, so we pray for ecclesial conversion. One strategy for our prayers is picturing them at the door and watching Jesus usher them into the pew beside us. Another strategy is to pray that God will send someone into their lives who will invite them to a nearby Catholic community. A third strategy is to pray for a son or daughter in a Catholic parish near their home. We also take a bulletin and pray for the particular parishioners who are responsible for

Baptism preparation, for weddings, and for reaching out to inactive Catholics in that parish. This is a way of acknowledging these people as our grown children's spiritual neighbors. Then it is time to let go of the results of our prayers.

Fr. Ron Rolheiser offers this thought as a source of hope for us—that as long as we love and forgive those who are away from the Church, we are keeping them connected in some way to Christ because we are his body:

> If someone whom you love strays from the church in terms of faith practice and morality, as long as you continue to love that person and hold him or her in love and forgiveness, he or she is touching the "hem of Christ's garment," is being held to the Body of Christ. . . . What Jesus did for us, we can do for each other. Our love and forgiveness are the cords that connect our loved ones to God, to salvation, and to the community of saints, even when they are no longer walking the path of explicit faith.[19]

A final strategy is to put our prayers into action by reaching out to young adults in our parishes. If we work at strengthening our own parish communities, then when someone else's adult child returns, we will not be found wanting. And if we reach out to someone else's grown child, we set a spiritual chain reaction in motion. The young person we touch may then touch the life of someone else, and that person may then touch the life of still another, until a total stranger reaches out and evangelizes our own son or daughter. So God often calls us to put our prayers into practice for the sake of the young adults around us who are ready for the embrace of the whole body of Christ. Here is what one young adult writes:

> We *are* present at your parishes, and our faith matters to us. We are at Mass on Sunday, even if irregularly. We are getting married in Catholic churches. We are bringing our children to be baptized and catechized in the Catholic Church. We attend funerals and marriages of our relatives and friends in Catholic churches. We are volunteering . . . at our children's schools. . . . We seek guidance from faith-filled people not only at church, but also at parties, coffee shops, and other non-church gatherings. We yearn for someone to notice our hunger to belong. . . . All of these are moments ripe with opportunity to begin building relationships with us and to begin noticing that we are *already* a part of your communities.[20]

Hunger for a World Transformed by Love

We must admit that the hunger for spiritual community and the possible return to church life are what we want most for our children and grandchildren. But God has often challenged us to let go of that kind of conversion. Instead, God has called us to pay attention to other kinds of conversions in the lives of our sons and daughters, such as sociopolitical conversion. This is the most common type of conversion among young adults as they embrace a hands-on approach to giving. An example from our daughter Claire's life comes to mind. One December day, Claire's neighbor, Penny, noticed that Claire was crying as she pulled into her driveway on her way home from work. It seems that some of Claire's fellow teachers had complained about the presence of a Christmas giving tree in their lounge because they didn't believe that all of the children who would get the gifts had truly needy parents. Worst yet, they thought that some of the parents might even be lying about the state of their finances in order to get free gifts. But Claire would do anything to prevent a child from going without Christmas gifts, even if were just for one child. When Penny heard the whole story, she replied, "Claire, you take every one of those ornaments off that tree. St. Michael's Parish will take care of this." What a striking witness this neighbor offered! What an example of encouraging a call to sociopolitical conversion! What an invitation to see God's ability to multiply our limited human resources through parish life!

And God is able to provide you with every blessing in abundance. . . . He who supplies seed to the sower and bread for food will supply and multiply your seed for sowing and increase the harvest of your righteousness. (2 Corinthians 9:8, 10)

Many young people choose a variety of ways to make a significant difference in the world, either in person or online. This God-given desire brings them to the threshold of the mission of Jesus, who was sent to "bring good news to the poor, / . . . to proclaim release to the captives / and recovery of sight to the blind, / to let the oppressed go free, / to proclaim the year of the Lord's favor" (Luke 4:18-19). So we rejoice in a son's or daughter's efforts to serve others. We can thank God for their altruism and support their projects. We can also pray to specific saints who shared the call to serve the same populations that interest a grown child. We might pray to St. John Bosco (1815–1888), who cared for poor and homeless children, or St. Thomas Becket (1118–1170), who had a passion for political reform.

Together with these saints, we ask that God will use our grown children. We pray that they experience the presence of Jesus at their side, because it is only Jesus who can give them strength when they have nothing left to give. We pray for Jesus to invite them to a deeper reliance on the Holy Spirit, who heals, provides food for the soul, frees us from all the consequences of sin, and resurrects us all on the last day.

Driven by Virtual Hungers

In 1999 Therese traveled to see the relics of St. Thérèse of Lisieux (1873–1897) at St. Patrick's Cathedral in New York City. The church was filled to capacity. Outside there was a large sign welcoming the relics of St. Thérèse, and just inside the open doors were two oversized video screens so that everyone could see the wooden reliquary. Therese decided to mingle with a steady stream of young adult visitors in the vestibule. After a short time, a curious young woman approached her with a question. She was intrigued by the sign and by what she had seen on the video screen and asked, "Who is St. Thérèse, and what's in the box?" Therese shared a little about her friendship with the Little Flower and about this saint's love for Jesus. The young woman replied, "Thanks! I am so glad I came in." But what if there had been no large welcoming sign and no video screen inside the vestibule? Would this young woman have walked right out?

This experience illustrates the young adult's penchant for media as their primary means for spiritual searching. They use websites, apps, social networking, texting, blogs, e-mail, twitter, online video, online chats, and video conferencing to seek God. These "digital natives" are most intrigued by virtual answers to life's important puzzles. While previous generations shared about God while washing clothes down by the river or by gathering crops in a field, this generation searches for God online, pioneering new avenues of spiritual awareness. One striking example of changes wrought by technology appeared in a story in our local news-paper, *The Trenton Times*: "A world away, Dad welcomes new daughter." James Reed, who was stationed in Kuwait, had par-ticipated in the birth of his second daughter by way of a webcam in the delivery room and software from Skype. Such "Internet-attended" births are happening all over the country, leading the way in family videoconferencing.

So how do we respond to the importance of the Internet in the lives of our adult sons and daughters? Where is God in this online universe? How do we pray for sons and daughters as inhabitants of an online culture? Pope Benedict XVI challenges the whole Church to respond

with an informed and responsible creativity, to join the network of relationships which the digital era has made possible. . . . The web is contributing to the development of new and more complex intellectual and spiritual hori-zons, new forms of shared awareness. In this field too we are called to proclaim our faith that Christ is God, the Savior of humanity and of history, the one in whom all things find their fulfillment.[21]

For us, using communication tools such as Facebook, e-mail, Skype, and live chat gives us insight into the day-to-day needs of our sons and daughters. It makes our intercessory prayers more pertinent. For example, we could pray for our daughter when her cellar flooded or for our son when he was in a car accident (which we first found out about on Facebook). If you are already involved with your children through the Internet, brainstorm for ways to use their communiqués as prayer requests, or consider praying "aloud" in an e-mail message or Facebook entry. Here are some things we have done to respond to this challenge. (If you are not online, ask a son, daughter, or friend to help you take our Internet tour at the end of this chapter for spiritual possibilities.)

- Share the Church's presence through links to websites (see the resource list in the back of this book).
- Explore issues like the relationship between technology and family life. A good place to start would be with an article entitled "How Technology Is Influencing Families."[22]
- Share about the meaning of current events for both generations (like Pope Benedict's conversation with astronauts in space).[23]
- Post old (but not embarrassing) family photos on Facebook or photo websites like Shutterfly or Flickr, where you can create a "family share site." We have found many cousins and nieces this way, like Brian, who responded to his mother's photo on

our Facebook page in this way: "The time when she died was the longest two days of my life, staying by her side till that moment. I miss her so much."

- Send or post religious e-cards on Christmas, Easter, and important feast days.
- For social networking, use Facebook to "friend" grown children. Offer encouragement about the events that they post on their wall. Therese once responded to Aunt Lillie's granddaughter, Brenda (from chapter five), who had a serious lung disease. After many months on oxygen, Brenda wrote, "I would like to be disconnected from this tank for one day, just one day!" Therese replied, "Pretend the tank is something else, like a suitcase full of tiny presents that you open one breath at a time."
- Offer prayers on Facebook when young people ask for help. Once when a sister-in-law asked for prayers for her husband's liver cancer, thirteen people responded with such encouraging messages as "You got it," "I'm with you," "Lord, have mercy," and "He's in our prayers."
- When engaged in a good chat or instant message, ask to switch to a telephone conversation.
- Share online music, including praise and worship songs.

If you feel any hesitation in learning these new forms of technology, be inspired by this challenge of Blessed John Paul II:

The Internet causes billions of images to appear on millions of computer monitors around the planet. From this galaxy of sight and sound, will the face of Christ emerge and the voice of Christ be heard? For it is only when his face is seen and his voice heard that the world will know the glad tidings of our redemption. . . . I dare to summon the whole Church bravely to cross this new threshold, to put out into the deep of the Net, so that now as in the past the great engagement of the Gospel and culture may show to the world "the glory of God on the face of Christ" (2 Corinthians 4:6).[24]

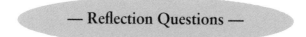

— Reflection Questions —

1. What is your experience of spiritual hunger and the search for meaning in your own life? In the lives of a son or daughter? How are the terms "spiritual" and "religious" connected or disconnected in your life or in the lives of young adults today?

2. What evidence do you see of a particular type of conversion in your son's or daughter's life—spiritual, Christian, ecclesial, intellectual, moral, or sociopolitical? Which type of conversion do you pray for most often, and in what ways?

3. In today's world, we have many options for communicating across time and space and across generations. Which is your preferred means of communication—telephone, letter, e-mail, texting, social-networking sites, or online chats? What is your adult child's preferred method? How do you compromise in terms of these preferences?

—Prayer Skill—
Part One:
Praying Your Way through the Creed

St. Ambrose (337–397) referred to the Creed as a "spiritual seal, our heart's meditation, . . . [and] the treasure of our soul."[25] A creed is a statement of our beliefs. What do you really believe about God? John's brother Bob prayed the first line of this "creed," in his own words, at his daughter's wedding supper: "God, I believe that you bless our families. And God, I thank you for the blessings we receive, day by day, hour by hour, minute by minute, whether we are aware of them or not. Amen."

Step One: Insert a grown child's name into the blank spaces. Then meditate on these personalized individual statements from the Apostles' Creed.

Step Two: Choose one line that strikes you. Repeat it a few times. Then put it into your own words or expand on it, as the Spirit leads.

I believe in God, the Father almighty, *my father and the father of my* _____.

[I believe in God] Creator of heaven and earth, *my Creator and the Creator of* _____.

And in Jesus Christ, his only Son, our Lord, *my Lord and Lord for* _____.

[I believe he] was conceived by the power of the Holy Spirit, *who also empowers me and offers his strength to* _____.

[I believe he was] born of the Virgin Mary, *my mother and the mother of* _____.

[I believe he] suffered under Pontius Pilate, was crucified, died, and was buried. *I know he was crucified for me and for my* _____.

[I believe] he descended into hell; on the third day he rose again from the dead, *for me and for* _____.

[I believe] he ascended into heaven, and is seated at the right hand of God the Father almighty, *where he prays for me and for* _____.

[I believe] from there he will come to judge the living and the dead, *and me and* _____.

I believe in the Holy Spirit, the holy catholic Church, the communion of saints, *my source of life, my true home, and the home of* _____.

[I believe in] the forgiveness of sins, *especially my sin of* _____ *toward my family.*

[I believe in] the resurrection of the body, and life everlasting, *for myself and especially for* _____.

Amen. *I believe! Help my unbelief!*

Part Two:
Internet Tour of the Spiritual Life

- Meditate with an online Taizé chant. (For an explanation of chanting, visit http://www.taize.fr/en_article338.html.)

  Bless the Lord
  (www.youtube.com/watch?v=t4Svh-9ohg4).
  Jesus, Remember Me
  (www.youtube.com/watch?v=xm3QC8vopO0).
  After praying this second chant for a while, substitute your grown child's name for "me."

- Meditate on the daily Mass Scripture readings at www.usccb.org.

- Explore spiritual websites that are young-adult friendly, such as www.bustedhalo.com, www.oncecatholic.org, or www.catholicscomehome.org.

- Try online giving that doesn't involve money, such as www.thehungersite.com/.

Chapter Seven

Praying When Our Adult Children Are in Danger

"It was May 2, 1983, and my son, Gerry, was in the middle of an earthquake in California," Shirley recalls. "I tried to call him on the phone. At first I couldn't get through, but when something like this happens to your son or daughter, you get very upset and you just need to speak to them. So I called the operator. 'Can you find a way to connect me to my son? He's in the middle of an earthquake.' Our phone carrier went through dozens of telephone lines and wires in Canada and every place while I prayed for God's help. Then I got through!"

Gerry remembers it this way: "Here I am, on the floor. I couldn't even stand up. Things had been thrown all over the apartment. And the telephone rings. I couldn't believe it! It was my mother."

Shirley adds, "He couldn't get over that. Nobody else could get through but me. I told the people at the phone company afterward that I really appreciated what they did. And I thanked God too!"

Dangers and afflictions of all kinds are part of the human condition. They happen to everyone. But when a tragedy threatens your son or daughter, it's a different story. Something inside of you becomes unhinged, and you are plunged into anguish. At times like these, you can draw great strength and hope from Jesus, who raised the widow's only son (Luke 7:11-17). Jesus was keenly aware of both the son's demise and his mother's imminent descent into poverty. He was moved by a dual compassion. Jesus "came forward and touched the bier, and the bearers stood still. And he said, 'Young man, I say to you, rise!' The dead man sat up and began to speak, and Jesus gave him to his mother" (11:14-15). Even now, Jesus understands and wants to touch both us and our children. And Jesus will give us back to each other in ways that we cannot even imagine.

In this chapter, we will consider several steps for surrendering to God's all-encompassing love for us and for our families during stressful, troubling times. It does not matter what kind of danger is involved; the steps are the same. First, call out to God. Second, ask yourself some important questions. Third, pray as a spiritual "first responder," and fourth, be prayerfully present to your troubled child in ways that reflect God's love.

"Out of the Depths I Cry to You, O LORD!"

This opening verse from Psalm 130 gives us a powerful image of praying from a deep and primal place when danger surrounds us. Our intense urge to cry out in pain does not need any explanation; we are all too familiar with this urge. But do we cry out to God or to someone else? How do we speak with God when something unspeakable is happening to a loved one? How do we cry out to God in ways that bring relief and enable us to offer assistance? Raw pain is an important gift to offer God in prayer. Jesus himself cried out to his Father on the cross (Matthew 27:46).

We suggest the following prayer strategies. Any one of them can be both helpful and fruitful. Whatever you choose, the goal is to place yourself before God so that Jesus can touch you in the way that you most need.

- Pray a single word like "Jesus" or a simple phrase like "The Lord is my shepherd" or "Let your face shine upon _____ (*name*) right now." Repeat your chosen phrase for several minutes.
- Sing a line from a hymn or a whole hymn repeatedly.
- Listen to religious music.
- Describe your child's need to a friend. Then ask your friend to pray an Our Father with you.
- Place your child on a prayer chain.
- Pray a Rosary.
- Hold a crucifix or a prayer card and tell God your feelings.
- Use a spiritual gift like the charismatic gift of tongues.
- Cry in God's presence at a nearby church, especially one in which there is perpetual Eucharistic adoration.
- Walk in a quiet place where you can talk to God aloud.

At one time, Therese was struggling with bone pain that radiated from the core of her body. As she prayed, she had a vision of the crucified Christ. At first she saw a small crucifix off in the distance, surrounded by total blackness. Then she was brought closer and closer, until she saw the details of Jesus' tortured body, the wood of the cross, and the black void that engulfed him. Finally, she was brought close enough to see that each minute detail of Christ's body was made up of many cubicles. Each detail contained someone who was suffering—a patient in a hospital bed, a worker with a heavy load, a woman in labor, a boy lost in a desert, a tearful funeral. There were thousands of people overcome with grief. Then a voice spoke out: "Will you join them? Will you unite your pain with theirs? Will you accept their pain and the pain of Jesus as your own, or will you suffer alone?" It was time to make a decision.

Ask Important Questions

Each of us faces a very primal choice when a loved one is in danger: "Will you offer your pain and your life for this loved one?" Most of us will answer, "Yes! He is my flesh and blood. Take me instead, God!" This grace is part of the fabric of parenthood. But there is a second crucial choice. Will you acknowledge Jesus as the one who is best equipped to handle your grown child's danger? Will you run to our heavenly Father and bring your child to him?

When you do, the Holy Spirit will help you get your bearings and sort out the answers to some very important questions: What is the immediate danger, and to whom? How is God present in this dangerous situation? What are my grown child's options for handling it? How can I be present to my son or daughter while he or she copes with the situation? What can I do as a parent? One author compares answering such questions to diagnosing a pilot's crisis.

> Test pilots have a litmus test for evaluating problems. When something goes wrong, they ask, "Is this thing still flying?" If the answer is yes, then there's no immediate danger, no need to overreact. When Apollo 12 took off, the spacecraft was hit by lightning. The entire console began to glow with orange and red lights. There was a temptation to "Do Something!" But the pilots asked themselves, "Is this thing still flying in the right direction?" . . . [And since it was,]

they let the lights glow as they addressed the individual problems, and watched the orange and red lights turn off one by one.[26]

In today's world, there are a host of serious problems that can threaten a loved one, and unfortunately, they can also happen in rapid succession while a grown child is living hundreds of miles away from us. A partial list of dangerous problems would include the death of a spouse or child, divorce, a serious illness or injury, job loss, prolonged unemployment, drug or alcohol addiction, catastrophic debt, and wartime military service. Every one of these situations makes it difficult for a son or daughter to function. Every situation precipitates a rapid-fire series of questions and disturbances in the family system. But God will give you the strength to tackle these questions, one by one.

Pray as a "Spiritual First Responder"

God is our refuge and strength,
    a very present help in trouble.
Therefore we will not fear, though the earth should change,
    though the mountains shake in the heart of the sea.
(Psalm 46:1-2)

One of the most consoling—and challenging—steps you can take during a family crisis is to switch gears from knee-jerk responses to ongoing prayer as a "spiritual first responder."

It's very important to choose simple acts like kneeling to pray, reading the psalms, or visualizing what Jesus might do. Resist the temptation to think that when you are "just" praying, you are not *doing* anything to help. This is not true. Prayer puts us in touch with the power of our Creator and our Redeemer and unleashes the breath of God's own Holy Spirit. So describe the details of the situation to God. No matter how foolish or impossible, God cares about every part of a crisis. Then imagine Jesus standing beside your child, doing whatever is necessary to help. Next, thank God for positive things about the situation. This is hard to do, but it will build your faith. Reading this prayer of Blessed William of St. Thierry (c. 1075–1148) is a helpful way to begin thanking God and placing your child in God's heart:

> We hold a gift more precious than gold, your love. From the beginning of creation your Son, the Eternal Word, has been tossing about on the stormy waters of human souls, striving to bring peace. . . . Now he breathes over the waters of our souls, and the waves are calm. Merciful Father, we thank you.[27]

Jesus prayed for his disciples often and sometimes became both a spiritual and a physical first responder. One day when he was praying, "He saw that they [the disciples] were straining at the oars against an adverse wind, [so] he came towards them . . . walking on the sea. [At first] he intended to pass them by" (Mark 6:48). Perhaps Jesus was just going to check on his friends the way a parent would tiptoe into a sick child's bedroom and listen for a moment. But the disciples panicked, and he stopped to assist them. God will also lead you to respond and be present to your daughter or son. And whether it is a daily phone call or a long-distance trip, you will need ever-increasing amounts of prayer as more needs surface.

So resist the temptation to stop praying or to accuse God of neglecting your loved one. God has not willed this problem. Tragedies, evil, and death do not come from God. They are a part of our fallen human condition. They are the by-products of sin and the consequences of our separation from God. We do know that God's goodness will triumph over evil and that human suffering is a mystery to be grappled with in prayer. Some dangers will be removed by God's healing presence. Others will not. Instead, God will give us strength to endure difficulties alongside our children, in the same way that Mary suffered with Jesus at the foot of his cross. As one author writes, prayer in times of intense darkness and suffering "shouldn't continue with your saying: 'God must have an intention here,' but rather with your saying: 'we are still in God's hands, even in grim situations like this one.' This terrible event isn't the last word. And you have to say that with all the strength that is in your being."[28]

God's Guidance for Self-Care

Let's return to the first questions that we suggested: What is the *immediate danger* and *to whom*? *How is God present* (to my adult child and to me) in this dangerous situation? Although it is tempting to focus all of your prayers on your grown child's needs, it is foolish not to seek God's help for yourself. As you pray, you must also identify your emotions, your greatest fears, your broken dreams, and even your motives for the assistance you want to offer. As you surrender all of this, God will give you the fruits and charisms you need to love your grown child in the name of the Father, the Son, and the Holy Spirit. You will actually become a sign of God's presence to your son or daughter.

Marion is a good example of paying attention to her own needs. When her grandchild was born with a heart defect, the baby's health crisis generated a host of fears in her. As she prayed, Marion discovered a larger fear underneath her immediate fears about the baby and her daughter. She was also afraid of how her son-in-law, a recovering alcoholic, might respond. Could she trust him? Could she even trust her own recovery as an alcoholic? She realized that she needed to return to her AA group and to a parish Renew group as well. This was her reasoning: "If I don't take care of myself the way I know how, then I will become part of the problem instead of being part of the solution. I just cannot trust God on my own. That doesn't work!" She was wise to name and identify her spiritual, emotional, and relational needs. If addressing your spiritual needs is a foreign idea, you can pray this Prayer for Christian Renewal:

Jesus, I know now that I am Yours and You are mine forever.
I thank You for sending Your Spirit to me
That I might have the power to live this new life with You.
Stir up Your Spirit in me.
Release Your Spirit in me.
Baptize me with the fullness of Your Spirit
That I may experience Your presence and power in my life.
That I may find new meaning in your Scriptures.
That I may find new meaning in the sacraments.
That I may find delight and comfort in prayer.

That I may be able to love as You love
    and forgive as You forgive.
That I may discover and use the gifts You give me
    for the life of the Church.
That I may experience the peace and the joy that You
    have promised us.
Fill me with Your Spirit, Jesus.
I wish to receive all that You have to give me. Amen.[29]

Issues of self-care can be most evident as you move toward action and come face-to-face with personal limitations due to age, finances, the needs of a spouse, or occupational responsibilities. So pray for God's wisdom and review the steps from chapter two. First, ask God to intervene in your daughter's or son's life [and yours]. Second, ask God to send the Holy Spirit as a guide and Jesus as Savior. Third, ask God for a clear understanding of the situation. Fourth, ask for God's help in choosing one detail to pray about. Fifth, choose to speak in ways that affirm a son or daughter. Choose one action or service that reflects God's love.

Respond in the Name of Love

When we find ourselves in some grave danger, we must not lose courage but firmly trust in God, for where there is the greatest danger, there is also the greatest help from Him who wants to be called our "Help" in times of peace and in times of tribulation.

—St. Ambrose[30]

At some point in your crisis-driven prayers, it is important to surrender your plans for helping. So let's return to the last three questions about giving assistance, since they are crucial considerations for a praying parent: What are my *grown child's options* for handling this? *How can I be present* to my son or daughter? *What can I do* as a parent? At first these questions may look like they are in the wrong order. But they are not. Remember, when a grown child is threatened, we are often catapulted emotionally back to the time when he or she was an infant, a toddler, or a schoolchild. This is normal. Bill had this experience when speaking with his son, Peter. Peter had just moved his family to a new city six months earlier and then lost his new job. Bill found himself saying, "You just get everybody in the car and come home!" Then he stopped himself, apologized, and said, "I am so sorry. I shouldn't be saying this. What are your options?" Bill was careful not to cross personal boundaries and rob his son of his dignity and responsibilities as an adult.

But it is good that Bill called Peter. Parents can be a source of real comfort and support as their grown children tackle their problems. You can always listen. You can always tell them what you hear them saying. You can increase the times that you are present to them. (Once or twice a day is a good interval during a crisis.) You can encourage your son or daughter by helping them list their needs and their personal resources during a crisis. You can help them connect with support from family and professionals. It is one of a parent's most precious gifts to support an adult child with all of these simple acts of mercy.

Since this book is about prayer and not about parenting per se, we suggest using an adaptation of the corporal works of mercy

(Matthew 25:40) as a guideline for your prayer when a daughter or son is in danger. The following list offers a gospel-centered yet objective approach for our actions. Keep in mind that in the early centuries in our Church's history, these works of mercy were first seen as being the actions of Jesus Christ toward us. He is the one who enters our chaos and takes every danger upon himself. Out of this understanding, our goal for each action becomes expressing our love as firmly rooted in the loving presence of Jesus to our families.

- During hunger: What hunger is my child facing? How can my child feed this hunger? How might I be present or offer food?

- During every kind of drought: What thirst is involved? How can my child quench this thirst? How might I be present or be of assistance?

- During homelessness: What part of "home" does my child need most? How can my child find shelter? What kind of shelter might I provide?

- During sickness: How can my child bring healing into the situation? How can I convey the healing presence of God? How might I visit?

- In prisons of every kind: How can my child move toward new freedom and hope? How might I reflect the freedom and forgiveness of God?

- In death: How can my child most effectively grieve and bury the dead? How might I be like Mary at the foot of the cross?

Here is an example of a parent who got creative about assisting during a grown child's illness. Angela's daughter broke her arm. It was a serious break and required a cast for several weeks. Angela wanted to help with laundry but could not because of the chronic bursitis in her shoulder. So Angela gave her niece, Pam, a ride to her daughter's house twice a week so that Pam could do the laundry. After three weeks of helping with rides, Angela took both of them out to lunch. So remember, coordinating services is an important role in family life, and you do have the ability to empower others. Search out creative ways for your family to offer God's mercy together. Consider ways of being signs of the resurrected love of Jesus together.

I see an infinite number of crucified persons in the world, but few are crucified by the love of Jesus. Some are crucified by their self-love and inordinate love of the world, but happy are they who are crucified for the love of Jesus; happy are they who live and died on the cross with Jesus.[31]
—St. Jean Eudes (1601–1680)

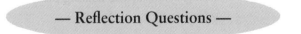

— Reflection Questions —

1. What kinds of dangers have wounded members of your family? What serious difficulties have touched the lives of your grown children? What impact have these troubles had on you? What could be done to surrender these troubles to God?

2. Choose one or two of the following images on suffering from the psalms. How do they touch upon your experience of coping with difficulties? What is it like for you to pray in the midst of suffering? What do these images mean to you as a praying parent?

- I am weary with my moaning; / every night I flood my bed with tears. (Psalm 6:6)

- Why are you cast down, O my soul? (Psalm 42:5)

- I cry by day, but you do not answer; / and by night, but find no rest. (Psalm 22:2)

- How long must I bear pain in my soul, / and have sorrow in my heart? (Psalm 13:2)

- My bones burn like a furnace. . . . / I eat ashes like bread. (Psalm 102:3, 9)

- In the night my hand is stretched out . . . ; / my soul refuses to be comforted. (Psalm 77:2)

- I am like those who have no help, / like those forsaken among the dead. (Psalm 88:4-5)

- You have made us the taunt of our neighbors, / the . . . scorn of those around us. (Psalm 44:13)

- My strength [is] dried up as by the heat of the summer. (Psalm 32:4)

3. Family tragedies often drive us to our knees. But do they leave us there? How do we do more than just survive a crisis? How do we gain strength from God in the midst of suffering? Which line in the Prayer of Christian Renewal in this chapter describes what you need most when difficulties challenge your faith?

—Prayer Skill—
Writing a Personal Lament

The word "lament" comes from a Latin word meaning "to howl" or "to mourn loudly." Psalms of lament give voice to a broad array of human suffering. Some psalms literally groan and wail. Some moan about personal terror. Some whimper. And even though some laments sound like a feverish mind gone awry, they are also acts of faith because they are addressed to God. Some psalms also go a step further by moving beyond complaints and into statements of trust in God.

Step One: Choose one of these laments: Psalms 13; 22:1-11; 42:1-5; 88:1-12; 130; or 142. Pray this psalm aloud and slowly. Then pray it again.

Step Two: Recall a difficulty that a grown child is facing. It can be anything, large or small, that absorbs your thoughts and moves you to the edges of worry and fear. Now bring this difficulty into God's presence by writing your own lament.

Greeting (or title for God):

_____

Describe the threatening situation in a few words:

_____

_____

Step back. State God's point of view (a scriptural image or a statement from the Creed):

_____

_____

Ask God for help. Then end with a surrender prayer:

_____

_____

Step Three: Choose a psalm of trust and thanksgiving: Psalms 16; 23; 34:1-10; 91:1-10; 124; or 145:1-13. Pray it slowly while you imagine your son or daughter beside you.

CHAPTER EIGHT

PRAYING FOR A SENSE OF VOCATION FOR OUR ADULT CHILDREN

Our son Charlie struggles to make a living as a freelance stained-glass window artist. One of his frustrations is estimating production time for a piece so that he can charge enough to make a living wage and support a family. Another frustration involves the tedious task of cleaning and restoring old church windows. One day while sharing these struggles, especially the demands of restoration, he told John, "Why should I continue? Why bother? Maybe the artists in my field who describe restoration work as 'polishing old turds' are right!"

John replied, "Well, Charlie, it must be hard to appreciate your own work when your colleagues demean it. But you should know that when I look at your stained-glass windows, I see a reflection of the incredible gifts God has given you! I feel as if I am gazing into the souls of the saints you portray. And as I marvel at the interplay of light and darkness, I am ushered into prayer."

John shared his appreciation of our son's work because he wanted Charlie to find new hope in his gifts. We share Charlie's struggles with you because they echo many young people's concerns about being engaged in much more than an occupation. They want to make a difference and leave their mark on the world. They admire people with radical commitments based on a strong sense of purpose. Our son Stephen, for example, admires an eighty-year-old ethnobotanist who has dedicated his life to studying plants and their uses in local cultures.

At the root of this desire for meaningful employment and a life filled with purpose is God's dual invitation to serve others through work and to follow Jesus through a particular "state in life." Appreciating these two callings is a good beginning point for us as praying parents. We can do this in several ways:

- Pray in thanksgiving for a son's or daughter's particular talents as they have unfolded in each one's life.
- Explore the rich meaning of the word "vocation" as it applies to both careers and to what the Church calls a "state in life."
- Offer prayerful support for grown children as they live the call to a single life, to marriage, to religious life, or to the Sacrament of Holy Orders.
- Watch for evidence of God's future invitations in the arena of work and in the area of a state in life.

The Call to Meaningful Service

Why do you spend your money for that which is not bread,
    and your labor for that which does not satisfy? . . .
Incline your ear, and come to me;
    listen, so that you may live. (Isaiah 55:2, 3)

During recent economic difficulties, many of us—young and old alike—have been reduced to praying for *any* job instead of *the* job. And whether your grown child is establishing himself as an adult or suffering from a midlife crisis, worries about finding, starting, and keeping a job can take a toll. Work issues have diminished self-esteem, taxed support systems, and raised questions about the meaning of life. Susan V. Vogt's informal study of several hundred young adults cites concerns about work as more pressing than any other issue.[32] So especially during the earlier stages in life, our children need our prayers and our vision of them as having important gifts to offer the world.

We can cultivate a new appreciation of a son's or daughter's talents by thinking back to the day they were confirmed. Through this sacrament, your daughter or son was anointed for a unique mission in life, a mission often lived out in the world of work. With that anointing, your son or daughter has been sent to "be who God meant you to be" and, by doing so, to "set the world on fire," as the Anglican bishop of London, presiding at the wedding of Prince William and Kate Middleton, reminded millions of young people who were watching it.[33]

God calls our sons and daughters! And we glorify God by recognizing their gifts, both in prayer and in later conversations with our grown children. Prayer strategies could include listing a child's talents in your journal or praying with his or her résumé, surrendering each achievement and the skills behind it to God. Our recent prayers for our daughter Rose are an example:

Thank you for her gift of stitching, of mask making, of puppetry, of imagining and designing costumes, and of managing costume workers. Thank you for her hands, her heart, her appreciation of beauty, and her contribution to the prophetic nature of theater. Call her into the job you have in mind for her, where she can fulfill her vocation to share your beauty and your message with the world. Amen.

The more confident we become of a grown child's giftedness, the more we will be able to offer encouragement when that child hits rough spots like a long job search, a change in careers, or difficulties with working conditions. Our prayerful encouragement will lead to statements such as "I'm sure that you have a lot to offer, like your capacity to _____" or "I am grateful for the experience you have gained at _____" or "I know that God has an important job out there for you."

Affirming Life's BIG Choices

I appeal to you therefore, brothers and sisters, by the mercies of God, to present your bodies as a living sacrifice, holy and acceptable to God, which is your spiritual worship. (Romans 12:1)

Often in parishes, the word "vocation" appears with a capital "V" and refers only to God's call to the priesthood or religious life. But let's explore this word from a broader perspective. While we certainly need priests and religious, what we need most is the realization that every baptized adult has a "Vocation"—whether it is the vocation of marriage, the vocation of the single life, the vocation of a vowed religious life, or the vocation of priesthood. So your son or daughter, as a baptized person, has a vocation. And God is calling your children to one of these choices. The Holy Spirit will give them the capacity to recognize God's inner voice despite the undertow of secularism, materialism, and relativism that surrounds them. The Holy Spirit can counteract other voices and give them the willingness to spend themselves for God.

As we pray, we can also examine our attitude toward *all* of these vocations and let go of any prejudices. All of these choices, when lived out in God's presence, are paths to holiness and love. Each option can shape a son's or daughter's life, like a pan that gives shape to a loaf of bread or an arrangement of girders that gives shape to a building. All of these choices are opportunities for intimacy, for successful relationships, and for a happy life. All of these choices can reflect Jesus, who is the light of all worlds. Just as you were entrusted with the light of the paschal candle at Baptism, you can prayerfully seek the light of wisdom for your grown children as they move toward marriage, a single life, or a religious vocation.

"But wait a minute!" you might say. "My daughter is living with someone and doesn't even want to get married, and certainly not in the Church." Or you might be thinking, "My son sees being single as a curse!" or "My children could care less about their 'state in life.'" How do you pray for a daughter's or a son's vocation under these circumstances? We hear you! And God hears you even better than we do! So listen to the advice that St. Vincent de Paul (1581–1660) gave to a distraught mother about her son's vocation.

> You tell me that your son's choice is God wreaking his justice on you. It is quite wrong to think like that. . . . Remember once and for all that bitter thoughts come from the evil one and sweet and tender thoughts from our Lord. . . . Let God guide him. God is his Father, more than you are his mother. . . . Leave God to arrange matters; he can call him later if he wants, or give him something else to do that will save his soul.[34]

Apparently, this mother listened. Today we know this woman as St. Louise de Marillac (1591–1660). And not only did she work out her anxieties about her son, but she also discovered her own vocation in the process of praying for him.

Single but Not Alone

A vocation that many young adults already experience is the single life. But they need to know that this vocation is not like the default setting on a computer or, worse yet, a consignment to loneliness. The single life can be inspiring when embraced for the sake of serving others in the name of Jesus. You may recall an aunt, uncle, teacher, friend, or associate who lived the single life out of love for God and others. Remembering such people can inspire you to look at a grown child's potential for serving others as a single adult. Thanking God for these people can bolster your appreciation for the meaningful activities of your single son or daughter. Our grown children are truly "sent" into daily life to make Jesus Christ and his gospel come to life.

Agnes remembers Mr. Price, her middle-school teacher. "The one thing that always stands out is how he went to church every day and shared that with our class. During the Easter season, he gave the entire class a prayer card. I carried that card in my wallet until my wallet was stolen in 1989. Of all the things that I lost in my wallet, that prayer card was the one thing I miss and that could never be replaced. I share his story often with my grandchildren."

In addition to thanking God for those who have lived out a single vocation, we can pray to one of the many single saints. One such saint is Blessed Pier Giorgio Frassati (1901–1925), an energetic young man from Italy who climbed mountains, helped the poor, enjoyed practical jokes, and lived his life centered on the Eucharist. Another is Blessed Josepha Naval Gerbes (1820–1893) from Spain, who taught needlepoint, spiritual reading, and prayer. St. Joseph Moscati (1880–1927), a single layperson who was an Italian doctor, biomedical researcher, hospital administrator, and medical school professor, often reminded his students of the perspective they should have regarding their own vocation:

> Only one science is unshakeable and unshaken, the one revealed by God, the science of the hereafter! In all your works, look to Heaven, to the eternity of life and of the soul, and orient yourself then much differently from the way that merely human considerations might suggest, and your activity will be inspired for the good.[35]

Finally, ask God to purify your own attitude toward the single life as a vocation. Therese's perspective was changed when one of our sons explained the following to her:

> Being single is an opportunity to give more time to family and friends, to listen in a different, more attentive way, because you are not invested in someone on a continuous basis. And for me, it's not helpful to think of being single as just a temporary condition. Because then you don't embrace the present moment. In the end, it's not whether it is temporary or permanent that is important. It's what you do with being single that matters. It's not a problem or a lack of something. It's a gift through which you can love and serve.

Calling All Married Couples

The most common vocation for our daughters and sons is a call to marriage. But in today's world, understanding marriage as a vocation is a countercultural activity. So let's consider a scriptural model first, the marriage of tentmakers Aquila and Priscilla, who met St. Paul in Corinth (Acts 18:2-3). They opened their home to him and provided a gathering place for the community at Ephesus (1 Corinthians 16:19). They also accompanied Paul on his return to Antioch (Acts 18:18). As you read about them, you will realize that the culture in which they lived was not that different from our own. So take heart, even when lifelong marriage is suspect and cohabitation is routine. Pray for your sons and daughters, especially when they are disillusioned about marriage. Have courage when the purpose of marriage and its nature as being between a man and a woman are questioned by your own children and loved ones. God is with us.

And furthermore, God is the creator of our sexuality. God cares when our grown children are caught up in sexual confusion. God's merciful response is the gift of sacramental marriage, a gift of abiding spiritual, emotional, and sexual friendship. The Father wants to bless couples with a refreshing stream of eternal love at the heart of married life. Jesus makes faithfulness possible. This vision is the Catholic parent's reference point in prayer. This is what God wants for our children. This is the gift that we must beg God to give, even as we watch our grown children struggle through the trauma of divorce or the many serious risks associated with cohabitation.

"God is love and in himself he lives a mystery of personal loving communion. Creating the human race in his own image . . . , God inscribed in the humanity of man and woman the *vocation*, and thus the capacity and responsibility, *of love* and communion." (CCC 2331, quoting Pope John Paul II's apostolic exhortation *Familiaris Consortio*, 11)

Here are some steps that parents can take to prayer in the context of the very real sexual friendships and activities of our adult sons and daughters.

- When a son or daughter establishes a serious relationship with someone, adopt that person in daily prayer. Your prayer might also be guided by your grown child's response to these questions: What do you like about him or her? If you could ask God to give him anything in the world, what would you ask for? Such questions and responses can guide you in prayer.

- Offer the relationship, as well as both individuals, to God. Even though you might not understand the way they choose to live, even though you might not agree with their thinking about marriage and family, pray for the relationship between them. Forgive them if necessary.

- Meditate on God's presence in your marriage (or his healing presence during a divorce). Offer God your own marriage. Young people pay more attention to a witness than to a lecture.

- Contemplate earlier marriages in your family. Watch for manifestations of God's love in these couples. Be assured that God has been present in all these marriages. God has been in their kitchens, in their bedrooms, and in their workday worlds.

- Write a brief journal entry about each important family marriage, accompanied by a family photo, as described in the exercise at the end of this chapter.

Is There a Priest or Sister in the House?

But you are a chosen race, a royal priesthood, a holy nation, God's own people, in order that you may proclaim the mighty acts of him who called you out of darkness into his marvelous light. (1 Peter 2:9)

Religious vocations may not be on a son's or daughter's radar, but God might have a different plan. And God has many ways of inviting a daughter or son into a religious vocation or into the priesthood. Venerable Solanus Casey (1870–1957) is an example. He was inspired to become a priest after witnessing a young woman's murder on the trolley tracks up ahead. Sr. Nancy was inspired by a college professor who kept asking her, "How is your soul today?" Blessed Miguel Pro (1891–1927) heard God's invitation when his two sisters chose to be nuns. So keep these possible vocations in mind, especially as you pray that a daughter or son experience ecclesial conversion and find his or her place in the Church.

Here are some steps you can take to pray for these vocations:

- Thank God for particular priests and sisters who have played an important role in your family. We thank God for Fr. Cy, who secretly donated part of his salary to start a family religious education program in our inner-city parish. We praise God for Fr. Gene, who shared many stories of his faith-filled pilgrimage to China with us.

- Pray for ecclesial conversion as described in chapter six.

- Pray for the needs of the Church—for priests, for sisters, for deacons, and for all lay ecclesial ministers. It is our passion for the needs of God's people that may open the door to religious vocations and to a wide variety of lay ministries.

- On a more personal note, interview older family members for stories about religious vocations in your extended family. Therese was surprised to find out that her grandmother's cousin, Joseph Comtois, had been a priest from 1887 to 1936. So she searched out family photos of him and took a picture of his grave to post on www.findagrave.com. Now Therese prays to Fr. Comtois that God might help those who are being called to religious life in our family.

- Ask God to show you the network of family vocations—the particular ebb and flow of married, single, and religious life—no matter how messy or dysfunctional. These vocations are meant to function like the background in the rich tapestry that is your family. Watch for ways that you can support and affirm the commitments between people. Watch for unique talents and vocations in grandchildren and stepgrandchildren. They need spiritual adoption and prayer. As they grow, watch for God's gifts and callings. Therese uses the following prayer that she discovered on one of Fr. Comtois' worn-out prayer cards to pray for several generations in our family.

Dear Jesus, lay Thy wounded hand upon my weary head,
And teach me to have courage in the paths that I must tread.
Bless me, and bless those whom I love. . . .
Bless my people, one and all, with Thy protecting grace,
And impart to them Thy wisdom
Ere they meet Thee face-to-face.

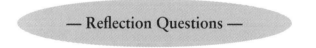

— Reflection Questions —

1. What is your understanding of the word "vocation"? When have you had a sense of being called by God? In what ways have you responded to God's call? What is your experience of using your God-given talents over the years?

2. What were some of the considerations in your decision to be single or to marry? What part did family and friends have in the process? How was God a part of your decision to build a family or to have children?

3. What evidence do you see of a son's or daughter's call to use their talents in service to others? What patterns seem to emerge as this son or daughter makes major decisions? What gives you hope about his or her state in life as a framework for these talents?

—Prayer Skill—
Photos as Pieces of Spiritual History

Step One: Look back on the (sacramental) marriages of your parents, grandparents, aunts, and uncles. List two or three married couples. Then add three good qualities about each relationship. How has God been present to each couple on your list? What witness do their lives offer to your family? Follow the directions below to meditate with a photo of one couple. (If you don't have such a picture, use a photo of just one of your parents or grandparents.) A sample exercise is provided below.

Step Two: After journaling, thank God for what you have discovered. Ask yourself these questions: With whom do I want to share this picture and the story behind it? What other photos might help me share God's presence in my family? Consider gathering five to ten photos and adding mini-stories for two or three, but don't go overboard with "spiritualizing" every photo. Consider keeping a diary or blog about your experiences as you meditate with family photos. You might also create a photo book (with text) or post and tag old pictures on Facebook. For more about sharing and preserving photos and the stories behind them, visit

"Seventeen Ways to Share Faith across the Generations" at www
.featurethat.com/faithsharing.html.

Opening Prayer

"Father in heaven, form us and transform us into the likeness of
your Son. Give us eyes to see your goodness in each other's faces.
Touch our hearts with your love so that we, in turn, may love
one another. Deepen your life within us, Jesus, especially when
we struggle together. Then send us as witnesses of gospel joy into
a fragile world of broken promises. We ask this through Christ
our Lord. Amen."

Discover God's Voice
in Family Photos

Start with the facts. Who is in the photo? What was the occasion?
Where and when? What happened before or after the photo was
taken? Try "story webbing" to delve into the *meaning* of your
photo. What word comes to mind? Draw a circle around this
word, and generate more words until a word or two strikes you
as a good beginning for a mini-story about the God-given qualities of your loved ones. Then answer the questions that follow.

Sample:
Harry and Claire Fenner

1. *How did they meet and decide to marry?*

It was 1939 when Claire began her job as a switchboard opera-tor at Northridge Furniture Company. She liked greeting callers, but she was unprepared for the young salesman who sauntered up to her one day and asked, "Why didn't they hire a good-look-ing blond?" His sense of humor certainly made an impression but not a favorable one. Still, he was persistent. So Claire invited him to tend the record player at several of her parties. We don't know when she changed her mind about him, but her little brother, Norman, noticed their budding love. One night he and a cousin crept behind the bushes to spy on them. The children were so intent on finding a good spot to watch them that they tripped and fell into a lake.

2. What place did God have in their marriage?

When Harry enlisted in the srmy in 1941, he first patrolled the coast in nearby Rhode Island, but then his unit was called up for service in the South Pacific. Harry and Claire wanted to marry before he left, but many relatives warned Claire that "you will be a pregnant widow if you do!" So Harry and Claire prayed a novena, and at the end, God reassured them that their love would survive the war. They married in February 1943 and made a pact to pray to St. Thérèse of Lisieux for Harry's safety. Then off he went into the South Pacific as a married soldier.

3. What were their unique gifts that point to God's love?

In gratitude for God's care and protection, Harry and Claire named their first daughter "Therese." She was the first of six children who were raised in a home shaped by faith in God. This faith was reflected in Harry and Claire's commitment to sing in the parish choir and in their willingness to take in family, such as Aunt Lillie or Claire's parents, whether it was for a few months or for several years.

CHAPTER NINE

PRAYING FOR THE ETERNAL HAPPINESS OF OUR ADULT CHILDREN

We have learned a lot about happiness from our little grandson, Edward. One Christmas while he was opening his gifts, he became intrigued by the crinkling sound of the gift wrap that Therese was scooping up from the floor. She noticed his curiosity and made even more noise. With a twinkle in her eye, she flung a handful of paper high up into the air and shouted, "Yippee!" Edward was totally enthralled. With another "Yippee!" and a "Yeah!" from Therese, Edward joined her in flinging paper with reckless abandon. Just as quickly, his mother, Ann, ran for her camera. And every Christmas or birthday after that has included a "Yippee bag" full of paper.

How much we desire to bring happiness to our loved ones! Think about how you stood before your Christmas tree in years past, your heart bursting with a love that spilled out over the brightly wrapped gifts. Think about the many Christmases, birthdays, and anniversaries you spent searching for the perfect gift that would make your loved one truly happy. And yet you wanted to give your family even more than those gifts. That desire is a tiny reflection of God's desire to lavish your children, and all of his children, with happiness beyond measure.

Now, here are two important questions about all those occasions. How often did you watch for the tiny God-given eruptions of spiritual delight beneath the ordinary human expressions of happiness? And how often did you acknowledge God as the ultimate source of a son's or daughter's deepest and most profound joy?

In this chapter, we will consider the ways in which God offers eternal happiness to our sons and daughters. We will outline ways in which different generations search for happiness and contentment in life. Then we will explore ways to pray for the happiness of our adult children and strategies for rejoicing in the Lord in prayer. And finally, we will consider ways to share our family's pilgrimage toward eternal happiness in heaven.

The Source of All Happiness

Ultimately, only God can offer total and eternal happiness. And only God can give us the grace to enjoy every small happiness along the way. So it is good to thank God for the joyful moments in your sons' and daughters' lives. It is like complimenting a good painter or a fine musician. So begin your prayers by acknowledging how God has already blessed your children and is leading them toward himself. Then examine the kind of happiness that you most want for your adult children and for yourself. Picture the unimaginable, eternal delight that God wants to give. Make eternal happiness in God's presence your point of reference and your goal as you pray for your daughters and sons.

Steve provides us with an example of how God can intervene in the pursuit of happiness. He and his wife valued friendship above many things, so one day God intervened in their friendships.

I decided to leave the Church because of a difficulty, and took my wife, Caroline, and our five children with me. But we did not know that our parishioner friends kept praying for our return. It took a visit with a dear Catholic friend,

Judy, who was dying of terminal cancer, for us to hear the Holy Spirit prompting us to come home to all of our friends in the Church. As we were driving home after visiting Judy, Caroline innocently asked, "If we were in this situation, what would we do?" After a short pause, we both answered in unison, "We would go back to the Catholic Church." And so we returned to the parish we had left. Later, when Caroline shared this great news with Judy's husband, he sobbed for joy because Judy had been quietly praying for our return throughout her illness.

Steve and Caroline had encountered God's incredible love, as did St. Maximilian Kolbe, which he expressed in this prayer:

Who would dare to imagine that you, O infinite, eternal God, have loved me for centuries, or to be more precise, from before the beginning of centuries? In fact you have loved me ever since you have existed as God . . . and precisely because you love me, O good God, you called me from nothingness to existence![36]

Steps toward God's Happiness

Pray to our incredible God for the total happiness of a daughter or son often. Consider using these steps.

Step One: Thank God for creating your son or daughter to enjoy his eternal happiness.

Step Two: Thank God for particular moments of happiness. Create a list of happy moments that you can refer to often. (For example, our son Charlie used to run and leap into John's arms, laughing all the way across the room. Our daughter Ann was so happy when she took her first steps that she laughed and cried at the same time. When our daughter Rose was a toddler, she took great delight in chasing seagulls.) Remembering those moments creates confidence in God's ability to help our grown children find true and lasting happiness.

Step Three: Ask Jesus to forgive you for times when you were an obstacle to God's happiness and love for your children.

Step Four: Tell Jesus that you trust him to bless your adult children with joy. And your trust, in the midst of difficulties, will release you from narrow prayers for little bits of happiness. Here is an example: "Oh Jesus, you alone know what will make my daughter happy and whole. You alone have set her on the path to eternal happiness in your presence, so do whatever you think is best. I ask only that you send her your Holy Spirit as I place her in your heart."

Hold onto the vision that each son or daughter has been created to enter and to reenter God's eternal joy, even at times when happiness disappears in a flash of bad news. This is why Jesus lived, died, and rose from the dead. This is why Jesus has come into our midst with good news of great joy. He is our hope for happiness. Jesus gives us the inner strength to survive all obstacles to joy. Jesus is the greatest evidence of the Father's particular love for each of us. He is the One who sends his Holy Spirit to offer our children unending joy. This is why the Scriptures and the Church invite us to rejoice in the Lord, especially in prayer.

The Holy Spirit gives us joy. And he is joy. Joy is the gift that sums up all the other gifts. It is the expression of happiness, of being in harmony with ourselves, which can only come from being in harmony with God and with his creation. It is part of the nature of joy to be spread, to be shared. The Church's missionary spirit is nothing other than the drive to share the joy that has been given to us.

—Pope Benedict XVI [37]

The Search for Happiness and Joy

During a recent car trip with one of our daughters, we compared notes on the pursuit of happiness. As we did, we realized that people of all ages seek out what makes them happy, whether that means eating ice cream, going for a run, spending time with friends, listening to music, watching a good movie, enjoying a quiet evening, or knowing that we are in a relationship of love that will last.

In addition, we are all surrounded by both invitations and obstacles to happiness from the people around us, from the advertising industry, or from the global world of the Internet. John recalled being happy about a cookout until he took a last-minute trip to the grocery store for mustard. His bubble was burst when he was faced with dozens of choices in the mustard aisle—sweet, Dijon, brown, honey mustard, yellow, and herbal—and didn't know which one to choose. They all seemed like obstacles on the road to a happy family cookout. Therese brought up the joy of taking a leisurely walk in the mall but then encountering the difficulty of passing up all the enticements to buy shoes, clothes, and snacks—an obstacle to her happiness. Like many people of our age, we both thought of the pursuit of happiness as a linear affair, a trip with stops or obstacles along the way.

But Rose sees the pursuit of happiness as being more like a spiral affair, with many exciting options that are part of the fun. For her, it is not a question of a linear road trip from point A to point B but a "loop-de-loop" in the stratospheres. Her examples included an evening with friends watching dozens of video clips from fifty years of filmmaking or an afternoon with a Wii console playing video games designed for three different kinds of systems.

This is an important distinction to keep in mind as we pray for our grown children. Our sons and daughters are more experimental in their search for happiness and in their beliefs about what brings happiness. One author categorizes many people in this age group as "tinkerers" (and "spiritual tinkerers") who "put together life from whatever skills, ideas, and resources are readily at hand. . . . When they need help from experts, they seek it. But they do not rely on only one way of doing things. Their approach to life is practical. They get things done, and usually this happens by improvising, by piecing together an idea from here, a skill from there, and a contact from somewhere else."[38] The differing points of view mean that our prayer for their happiness might feel like a balancing act. But this is normal.

There is a way to bring these points of view together in prayer. Begin with your young person's idea of happiness, acknowledge your definition of happiness, and then end with God's point of view. For example, one of our daughters was depressed about a broken pool pump. So we began by praying that she would find a good pump at a reasonable price, as she had requested. Then we went a step further and asked God to bless her family's time in the pool. We know how fast her children are growing up. We look at life from the long view because in the process of aging, we have pursued many avenues for happiness and rejected many dead ends. Finally, we asked God to intervene and multiply their joy by revealing his presence. That might happen through unexpected good weather, a visit from friends, or an impromptu celebration of a breakthrough at swimming lessons. That part is up to God.

God's Call to Rejoice

"My soul magnifies the Lord,
　and my spirit rejoices in God my Savior,
for he has looked with favor on the lowliness of his servant."
(Luke 1:46-48)

Mary uttered these words after her long trip into the hill country to visit her cousin Elizabeth. Like Mary, we are called to rejoice in God's gift of a son or daughter. It does not matter if their entry into our lives was unexpected or even unwelcomed. Each son or daughter is given to us as a gift, no matter what the circumstances. So choose to rejoice in prayer as Mary did. When you do, rejoicing in the Lord will widen your heart and dispel many difficult emotions, although it may take time. And accepting the grace of God to rejoice will become a spiritual key to your children's ultimate happiness. John has hung a four-foot-long banner in his office to remind him of that truth. It features a giant lavender cross with a golden sun at its center. At the base of the cross is a golden sunrise with the word "JOY."

> Rejoice always, pray without ceasing, give thanks in all circumstances; for this is the will of God in Christ Jesus for you. (1 Thessalonians 5:16-18)

Rejoicing does not mean conjuring up feelings. It is not a "grin and bear it" phenomenon. It means choosing Jesus as your happiness. It means praising God in the midst of troubles that you don't understand because Jesus is your eternal destiny. It means taking a sneak peek at what God has in store for you and for your children.

St. Thérèse of Lisieux comes to mind as an example. She chose to rejoice in the Lord despite the tuberculosis that wracked her body for the last eighteen months of her life. Her joy in Jesus was evident in the photos that her sister Celine took of her. One day, however, when the sisters complained that in a particular photo she was not smiling, Therese replied, "Be sure . . . that if my photograph does not smile at you, my soul will not stop smiling at you."[39]

Storing Up Treasures in Heaven

> Do not store up for yourselves treasures on earth, where moth and rust consume and where thieves break in and steal; but store up for yourselves treasure in heaven, where

neither moth nor rust consumes. . . . For where your treasure is, there your heart will be also. (Matthew 6:19-21)

St. Matthew's Gospel challenges us to look toward heaven as our destination and as the ultimate happiness for ourselves and our loved ones. This is no easy task when you are challenged by a son's doubts about the existence of heaven or by a daughter's belief in reincarnation. The truth is that all of humanity is on a pilgrimage home that began centuries ago with Abraham and continues through the centuries with a parade of saints. But we are not responsible for the decisions that our grown children make in the pursuit of happiness. So pray for them to surrender to the grace of God's invitation to seek the endless presence of Jesus.

He is so bright, so majestic, so serene, so harmonious, so pure; He so surpasses, as its prototype and fullness, all that is graceful, gentle, sweet, and fair on earth; His voice is so touching, and His smile so winning . . . , that we need nothing more than to gaze and listen, and be happy.
—Blessed John Henry Newman (1801–1890)[40]

Praying for the eternal happiness of your children can be compared to those times when they were young and you traveled with them to a far-off destination. "Are we there yet?" they would ask again and again. Then and now, it is your vision of their destination that makes all the difference between a happy and a miserable journey. So are your eyes fixed on heaven?

One woman's answer comes to mind, and it was a sad one. We met Alice at a workshop about God's mercy. She was very disturbed about her grown daughter's decision to live with a boy-friend. Alice finished her story by concluding, "And she is going straight to hell for this!" We acknowledged that her daughter's behavior was not in line with the gospel, but then we reassured her that God still loved her daughter. Alice couldn't hear us. She was sure her daughter would go to hell. We were just as convinced that Alice's condemnation and rejection of her daughter would do more to drive her daughter toward hell than toward heaven.

So look toward heaven, and be patient as our young people search out what heaven means. Be encouraged about their ability to seek and about God's ability to lead them. If you need convincing, listen to the popular song "I Can Only Imagine" by MercyMe on YouTube.[41] It describes the mystery of heaven and the experience of awe in God's presence. The good news is that this song has had more than sixteen million online "hits."

I Saw a Great Cloud of Witnesses

This perfect life with the Most Holy Trinity—this communion of life and love with the Trinity, with the Virgin Mary, the angels and all the blessed—is called "heaven." Heaven is the ultimate end and fulfillment of the deepest human longings, the state of supreme, definitive happiness. (CCC 1024)

For older people, grappling with the deaths of loved ones can potentially be a very spiritually enriching experience. We hope they are among the blessed in heaven. If we face the challenges of saying good-bye and burying them with prayer, God will enrich our vision of heaven. If we give them to Jesus, then their new lives in him will give us a new incentive to pray that our children reach their destination of heaven too. But this means surrendering despair, depression, and sometimes faulty attitudes toward death that are not grounded in the good news of the gospel.

It is important to remember that your grief over the loss of a loved one can bear fruit in your life. Your review of that person's life can become a new tool for sharing heaven with your adult sons and daughters. And you can use their story to share your family's unique pilgrimage toward heaven. So that your sons and daughters do not succumb to "spiritual amnesia," you can collect and share several stories of family members who have died in faith. We have often shared such stories through eulogies at family funerals, through posting obituaries and faith stories on www.findagrave.com, and through sharing printed eulogies on the anniversary of a family member's death. These stories are often the inspiration that our daughters and sons need to recognize God's invitation to find eternal happiness in him.

John's eulogy for his brother Lou began by his sharing about one of his visits after Lou had been stricken with Alzheimer's disease.

What struck me most was the moment Louie roused himself from a mini-nap, sat up straight, looked me in the eye, and said, "What are you doing here?" I thought about this question often in the year that followed because it reminded me of Louie's whole life and what that life said to me.

"What are you doing here?" Louie asked himself as a milkman and as a salesman. This question became all the more important after his involvement in the Cursillo movement, in the St. Vincent de Paul Society, and in prayer groups. Part of his answer to himself was to found Boucher's Good Books, where he could serve by providing Catholic books and music that would help people become disciples of Jesus Christ! It seems that this ministry got started because Louie had purchased so many copies of *My Daily Bread* to give away that the previous store owner remarked, "What are you doing here again? Why don't you just buy the whole store?"

So now as we bury Louie, I am asking you to consider this same question for yourself. What are you doing here today? Are you just honoring Louis A. Boucher? Are you just letting go of your brother, father, grandfather, or friend? Are you just celebrating one of us who is gone ahead of us to heaven? I hope not! I hope that you ask yourself Louie's question. What are you doing here? What are you doing to serve others and to show them the love of God in a practical way? What are you doing here on this earth right now—not just tomorrow, next week, next year, or whenever you get around to it, but right now—to come closer to Jesus?

Now we invite you to share your journey and the journey of your family members toward Jesus, toward heaven. Their pilgrimage is important. God will show you how to get started and will give you the strength to keep at this important task. Meanwhile, let us pray for our sons and daughters as they pursue happiness, a happiness that will last. In the words of one author, let us wrap our adult children in the arms of intercession and march them into the gates of heaven: "This is the inheritance we can leave our children—an inheritance of prayer, prayers lifted to God long before the children were born, prayers answered long after we are gone."[42]

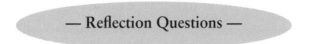

— Reflection Questions —

1. What brings happiness to your son or daughter? How has the answer to this question changed over the years? In what ways do you try to make them happy now? In what ways have you let go of control over their happiness?

2. What does God's invitation to rejoice mean? How could you surrender more fully to the Holy Spirit's gifts of joy, peace, hope, and goodness? What steps could you take to share God's joy with your loved ones?

3. What is your understanding of this statement from the new translation of the Nicene Creed: "I look forward to the resurrection of the dead and the life of the world to come"? How does this understanding reflect or challenge your family's experiences of death, loss, and heaven?

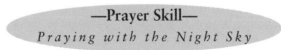

—Prayer Skill—
Praying with the Night Sky

This exercise was conceived after a conversation with our niece, who has a doctorate in astronomy. Although she had never really thought of praying with the stars, "I know I feel wonder and a big chill when I look up at the night sky and realize how huge it is," she told us. "I feel small and powerless yet amazed to be part of it all." Modern science tells us that we are made out of the stuff that was forged from the stars. As our niece explained to us: "We are 'children of heaven' in a quite literal sense."

Step One: Choose an evening when the sky is clear, the moon is barely visible, and you can be comfortable outdoors. Or choose a room with the best view of the sky and turn out all the lights. In either case, you will need a flashlight to read the following prayers:

Opening Prayer

"I thank you, Holy Father, for creating the sun and all the stars and for giving each star its name (Psalm 147:1, 4-5). I thank you for the planets, for the billions of galaxies, and for the whole vast universe and even its darkness. Your creation is beyond all human understanding and imagination. Help me appreciate the place you have prepared for me and for my family in your creation. Bless my children and all the generations of our family before us who have lived under your stars. Bless those after us who will live under your stars, Holy Father."

A Reading from Psalm 8

O Lord, our Sovereign,
     how majestic is your name in all the earth!
You have set your glory above the heavens . . .
When I look at your heavens, the work of your fingers,

the moon and the stars that you have established;
what are human beings that you are mindful of them,
mortals that you care for them? (verses 1, 3-4)

Step Two: Pray this litany to the saints:

Lord of the universe, I acknowledge your presence, your guiding hand. You promised Abraham descendants as plentiful as the stars and as numerous as the grains of shimmering sand at the ocean's edge (Genesis 22:17). I choose you as the Alpha and Omega, the beginning and the end, of all history, of all time and space, and of my family. I pray that each of my loved ones will find a place in the heavenly company of all the saints. I call out to these saints on behalf of my family.

Response: Pray for us. Pray with us for our sons and daughters.

Abraham and Sarah, you relied on God's promises for all generations and for all time. **R.**

St. Margaret Clithrow, you risked your life to share your faith with your children. **R.**

Mother of Zebedee's sons, you wanted more than the world could give for your sons. **R.**

St. Monica, family peacemaker, you were persistent in heroic prayer for your son. **R.**

St. Augustine, you found Jesus our Lord in the school of your mother's heart. **R.**

St. Elizabeth, mother of John the Baptist, you challenge us to prepare the way for Jesus. **R.**

Blessed Louis and Zelie Martin, you raised five daughters who gave themselves to God. **R.**

Blessed Marie of the Incarnation, you sacrificed being with your son for the sake of God's orphaned children. **R.**

St. Gianna Beretta Molla, you created a home where God was like one of the family. **R.**

St. Thomas More, you taught all of your children a love for God's truth. **R.**

St. Jane Francis de Chantal, you prayed, "Let your will be done in this family in everything that concerns us." **R.**

We thank you, Father, for hearing our prayers and the prayers of those who have gone ahead of us in faith. Show us and our loved ones the way home to heaven. We ask this through Jesus the Christ. Amen.

CHAPTER TEN

PRAYING FOR ONE ANOTHER'S CHILDREN

Connie's son, Michael, stormed out of the house carrying all of his clothes, a few of his favorite books, and his guitar. Then he moved into an apartment with a friend in a very questionable neighborhood. Connie's background as a visiting nurse in the area convinced her that he was in serious danger. So she called Therese and asked for her prayers. Therese took Connie's fear and her own to God. She asked Jesus to surround Michael, especially if he should be assaulted or attacked in any way. This prayer brought great peace. Still, Therese knew that she would feel even more relief when she could pray with Connie in person. Fortunately, Therese had made a reservation for an upcoming flight to her hometown, where Connie lived.

A few more days passed. Then Therese moved up the day of her flight in order to take advantage of a sale. When Therese's dad picked her up at the airport that afternoon, he told her the terrible news: Michael had been killed in a knife fight. Therese was shocked. Dad explained, "Michael was stabbed in the heart and should have died instantly. But he survived the ambulance ride to the hospital. Then, as he was being wheeled into the emergency room, a priest was passing by. The priest took Michael's hand, and they raced down the hall to the OR, praying for God's forgiveness for Michael. The last thing he said to the priest before he died was 'Tell my mother I love her.' And now, by the grace of God, Therese, you are here just in time for his wake. It's tonight!"

It took a while, but Therese began to see how God had led her in her prayers for Michael. He had survived long enough to speak words of love and forgiveness to his mother. God had brought Therese home in time to comfort her friend. Even more important, God gave Connie the grace to live in his mercy—first, by visiting and forgiving her son's killer in his jail cell, and later, by testifying against the death penalty.

Praying for one another's children happens naturally when people are friends, when they are brothers and sisters in Christ. Praying for one another's children becomes an essential part of sharing the journey of faith, especially when sharing the trials of dealing with obstacles to faith in our families. In this chapter, we will explore ways in which we can enlist each other's prayers through this important act of spiritual compassion. We will consider interceding for each other's grown children as part of our spiritual friendships or as members of faith-sharing communities. We will consider God's call to adopt young adults as spiritual sons or daughters. Then we will explore praying with the saints in heaven for our children. Finally, we will consider important steps that can follow intercessory prayer.

Enlisting the Prayers of Living Saints

St. Gregory the Great (c. 574–590) describes what can happen among us:

When we are linked by the power of prayer, we, as it were, hold each other's hand as we walk side by side along a slippery path; and thus by the generous disposition of charity [as we lean] on each other, it happens that the harder each one leans on the other, the more firmly we are riveted together in brotherly love.[43]

Praying for each other's children is often an essential part of a one-to-one spiritual friendship. Therese finds great strength in these types of friendships, especially when a friend is willing to spend regular time in prayer for one of our sons or daughters.

Marriage can also be this type of spiritual friendship. Husbands and wives praying for their children together can be a very effective part of the Sacrament of Marriage, especially when both spouses are willing to pray aloud together. Our prayers strengthen each of us so that we can better relate to our grown children. We pray this way often, believing that our prayers are the fruits of sacramental marriage.

Intercessory prayer is most successful when it is part of the fabric of the prayers of a small faith community. It could be the faith community that surrounded you when your child was baptized or when he or she received First Communion. It could be your current faith-sharing group, a ministry group in your parish, or a daily Mass community (even if you can go to Mass only once during the week). So explore these possibilities if you are not familiar with them.

If you want to start chronologically, you might ask your grown child's godparents or Confirmation sponsors to pray with you. They already have a unique call to intercede for your son or daughter. It is an integral part of their job description and their promise to support both child and parents. Through Baptism the lives of godchildren and sponsors are forever united.

> For the grace of Baptism to unfold, the parents' help is important. So too is the role of the *godfather* and *godmother*, who must be firm believers, able and ready to help the newly baptized—child or adult—on the road of Christian life. Their task is a truly ecclesial function. (CCC 1255)

John's older brother, Jerry, and his sister, Shirley, a religious who was a Sister of St. Anne, were his godparents. They both prayed for him on a regular basis through several illnesses in his childhood. Some years later, when Shirley left religious life to answer a call to marriage, she prayed that Jesus would call someone else in the family to serve the Church. When John decided to embrace full-time lay ministry, her heart leapt for joy! Every time she saw John at family gatherings, she would remind him of her constant prayers for him and of God's faithfulness in calling him to "replace" her in ministry.

Jerry, too, prayed for John and for our family throughout the years and was always ready to offer his support for our young family. More recently, when Jerry lay dying of cancer, he and John shared phone conversations on an almost weekly basis. At the end of each conversation, John would ask Jerry to pray for him and for our family. Knowing that each phone call might be their last, Jerry would always end by saying, "I have never stopped praying for you, and I never will." Then he would repeat a French Canadian father's blessing that translates this way: "Happy New Year, good health, and may you see Paradise at the end of your days."

Beyond the parents and godparents, the *Catechism* describes the crucial role of the whole faith community in supporting each other's children in faith: "The whole ecclesial community bears some responsibility for the development and safeguarding of the grace given at Baptism" (1255). So consider that your spiritual responsibility is to pray for each other's children. Consider a faith-sharing group, a Bible study group, a prayer group, or a Renew community where you can share the needs of your individual adult children. Of course, this kind of prayer requires confidentiality regarding the details of family situations.

The advantages of such prayer are many. Your brothers and sisters, your friends in Christ, can add hope and understanding to your intercessory prayer. Small-group members can help you see the ways in which God is answering your prayers. They can help you persevere in prayer simply by inquiring about a loved one's progress. They may notice blind spots in your life where you might fail to see what Jesus is doing or wants to do in your children's lives and struggles. And finally, they can be present in a crisis. Therese's friend Kathy shares the power of mutual support in a small faith sharing group.

In the mid-1970s, I was part of a women's morning prayer group where everyone developed strong relationships through prayer, Scripture, and sharing each other's insights and burdens. One morning when my husband was having chest pains, I called one of the members for help with the children so that I could go to the hospital with him. She arrived within a few minutes in her bathrobe and slippers. Her husband had driven her over as soon as she had hung up the phone. This was the most profound experience I ever had of God's personal love for me. I have tried to be part of a community like this ever since then.

The Grace of Spiritual Adoption

We are never more like Christ than when we are praying for others. Intercession is laying down our life for our friend; it is bearing one another's burden; it is sharing in the suffering of Christ. The work of redemption . . . is the work of intercession. Jesus is interceding, the Holy Spirit is interceding, and we are interceding.[44]

Sometimes God calls us to pray for someone else's son or daughter in a more intense way, perhaps because of some special circumstance. As an infant, John was the beneficiary of much intercessory prayer. His mother, Mary, suffered a near-fatal blood-clotting disorder that required several weeks in the hospital and then several more months of bed rest. So John was given to a young cousin Gertrude and her husband, who were unable to have children. Gertrude brought John to visit his mother often. But even more often, she held him in her arms and prayed for him, for his mother, and for a child of her own. John's earliest photos show her cradling him in prayer at Catholic shrines throughout New England.

For our part, we "spiritually adopted" one of our former babysitters named Debbie. At first this involved praying that she would do well in college. Later it meant asking God to help Debbie cope with a polio disability that made it difficult for her to drive, to marry, and to have children. But we watched God give her all of these things. More recently, we prayed about her struggles to find a church in which she and her wheelchair-bound husband could feel comfortable and grow in their relationship with Jesus. And now we also enjoy communicating with Debbie on Facebook and praying about the little things that crop up in her life on a day-to-day basis. We rejoiced when we saw that she had put this Scripture verse in her bio: "That they may see and know . . . / that the hand of the LORD has done this, / and the Holy One of Israel has created it" (Isaiah 41:20).

Surrounded by the Communion of Saints

Intercessory prayer for our children, both natural and adopted, is a calling that can be shared with our brothers and sisters in heaven. The litany of saints who prayed for us during family Baptisms and the family saints who have gone ahead of us in the Lord always stand ready to befriend us throughout the trials of our adult children. By knowingly bringing our children to these saints in prayer, we acknowledge the die/rise/reign cycle of new life in Christ that these saints have already perfected. We embrace our common destination in Jesus. The *Catechism* reminds us how readily we can and should ask family saints and canonized saints to pray with us:

They contemplate God, praise him and constantly care for those whom they have left on earth. When they entered into the joy of their Master, they were "put in charge of many things" (cf. Matthew 25:21). Their intercession is their most exalted service to God's plan. We can and should ask them to intercede for us and for the whole world. (2683)

So ask a saint to pray with you. Ask your patron saint, a family saint, a saint with your ethnic background, a saint who was a parent, or a saint with the same occupation or issues as your grown child.[45] If we were to pray on the basis of our daughter Claire's vocation, we would say, "Blessed John Paul II, great teacher of the Faith, intercede for our daughter Claire as she teaches God's children." We also pray to saints who are spiritually associated with our sons and daughters based on their dates of birth. Ann was born on the feast of St. John Vianney; Rose, on St. Padre Pio's feast; Charlie, on St. John Eudes' feast; and Stephen, on St. John Neumann's feast day. Claire was born on Christmas Eve, when we celebrate the day that Mary gave birth to our Savior, Jesus Christ. And, of course, we pray for all of our loved ones with St. Thérèse of Lisieux, who always included her family in her daily prayers:

O my God! I ask of you for myself and for those whom I hold dear, the grace to fulfill perfectly your holy will, to accept for love of you the joys and sorrows of this passing life, so that we may one day be united together in heaven for all eternity. Amen.[46]

Prayer as a Stepping-Stone to Sharing Faith

For many, intercessory prayer is the doorway to a greater call to share Jesus in every way possible. Prayer becomes the first of four steps: prayer, care, share, and dare to invite. A conscious desire to follow these steps is the forerunner for bringing the good news of Jesus into every situation, or what is called "evangelization." Through a conscious effort to take these steps, we imitate Jesus, who prayed often, cared by healing others, shared what he knew about the Father, and dared to invite others to faith, such as the rich young man and the fishermen who became disciples.

The following description of these evangelizing activities is adapted from our book *When You Notice the Empty Pews: Simple Ways to Share Our Faith.*[47] Like Jesus, we can enter the same cycle of prayer, care, share, and dare to invite. More often than not, we begin with the quiet, caring witness of everyday life. Then, as we become more and more grounded in prayer, we notice opportunities to take a few more steps. God's Holy Spirit lights the way and provides new ways to fill empty hearts and empty pews.

Prayer: Evangelizing intercessory prayer is driven by a desire to recognize Jesus at work in our daily lives and in our communities. We watch for God's presence and for concrete opportunities to connect and reconnect people to Jesus from within and beyond our families. As we pray, Jesus gives us new compassion and fresh insights about how God might address the unmet needs of the people around us. John's decision to play online chess with our son Stephen was the fruit of this kind of prayer.

Care: Being sensitive to people's needs is the never-ending task of the follower of Christ. We care through compassionate listening and through acts of service. We care through addressing issues of social justice that affect our families. Our goal is to make God's love incarnate and even global. We participate in God's particular love for someone, expecting God to intervene and multiply our resources. We offer a witness to Jesus Christ, who is the ultimate answer to all human needs. The couple in chapter two who provided a home for Alice and her toddler is a good example, and so is Angela in chapter seven, who provided rides so that her daughter's laundry would get done.

Share: The Scriptures also invite us to be ready to share what we have experienced of God. This happens most easily with other people's children and is used sparingly with our own. Simple questions like "How are you doing?" can be used to search out spiritual hungers and to have conversations that include appropriate faith stories. Doing so can energize our relationship and focus our attention on spiritual caring. Therese's Facebook sharing about Brenda's oxygen tank in chapter six is an example.

Dare to Invite: Blessed John Paul II often proposed these questions: "What have I done with my Baptism?" and "How have I shared it?" Baptism is not a private sacrament but the opening of an inner door beckoning us to live our faith together. We can open this door by calling others to new or deeper encounters with God in our families and faith communities. Saying grace on holidays is one example. The grandfather in chapter four who invited his children to pray the Rosary is another.

Individuals and whole parishes can also invite others to faith. Here is one example: Not too long ago, Eric contacted John through a series of e-mails. He and his wife, Kaitlin, were expecting their third child and wanted to return to the Catholic Church after a fifteen-year absence. They wanted their marriage blessed and their children baptized. After a lot of prayerful listening, John asked permission to arrange contact between Eric and a pastoral associate named Beverly from a parish near Eric's home. Then John told Beverly about these young adults who longed for a spiritual home. Beverly gave John her e-mail address, and he passed it on to Eric.

After a few months, John sent a follow-up e-mail to Eric. And yes, their marriage had been blessed. Their new baby, Joshua, had been born and baptized. But only four weeks later, the baby died of pneumonia. The parish bereavement ministry had stepped in to offer crucial ongoing support in several ways. Eric told John, "We are so grateful to be home in the Catholic Church. We are struggling, but we are being constantly bathed in the prayer and love of our brothers and sisters in Jesus Christ!"

Perhaps Eric's or Kaitlin's parents had been praying for them, or perhaps an uncle or a friend had. It doesn't matter who or how or even when this prayer may have happened. What matters is that God is inviting each of us to enter into his presence often so that together we can lift up our sons and daughters, nieces and nephews, and all the young adults around us. Together we must become a generation set ablaze with the transforming love of Father, Son, and Holy Spirit, calling out to those who come after us.

We cannot keep to ourselves the words of eternal life given to us in our encounter with Jesus Christ: they are meant for everyone, for every man and woman. . . . It is our responsibility to pass on what, by God's grace, we ourselves have received.

—Pope Benedict XVI[48]

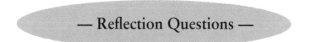

— Reflection Questions —

1. How could parishes and individuals promote a deeper appreciation for the communion of saints? What saints do you find to be appealing? Why?

2. What is it like for you to ask others for prayer? How do you respond when others ask you to pray? How might your experiences be different after reading this book?

3. How does prayer empower you to reach out to others? Which is easiest for you—offering a caring witness, sharing times when God has been with you, or inviting young adults to gatherings of your faith community? Why?

—Prayer Skill—
Meditation on a Kitchen Table and an Altar

This exercise is designed to help us get in touch with significant impressions and memories of family life and parish life. Use a plain piece of paper to recreate your family table when everyone was still at home. Draw a shape for each person. Then assign a particular color for that person. If you do not have crayons or markers, write the name of the color next to his or her name.

Family Table Drawing

Step One: Draw a large shape to represent your family table *when your children were young.* Use a shape (and a color) for each family member seated around the table. Add items from a favorite meal on the table. Then add an extra place for Jesus.

Step Two: Share your responses to these questions:

- What does the phrase "family table" bring to mind?
- What does your drawing tell you about some of the individuals?
- What was your experience of being together as a growing family?
- How was Jesus present to your family at that time?

Parish Table Drawing

Step One: Draw a large shape for *your present-day parish altar,* with a shape or symbol for Jesus in the center of the altar. Add a few wide pews. Use shapes to represent a few people with whom you worship. Add people you pray for on a regular basis as well as your grown children (and perhaps their children), whether they are regular churchgoers or not.

Step Two: Share your responses to these questions:

- How is your worship experience like or unlike the gathering of a family or the gathering of the communion of saints?
- Who is present around you during Sunday Mass?
- What is your experience of praying for your loved ones during liturgies?
- How have the worship decisions of your adult sons and daughters affected you?

Step Three: Spend a few minutes praying for each of your adult children. Begin by visualizing Jesus in the center aisle. Thank him for each one by name. Then visualize Jesus greeting each one and bringing them forward to sit beside you in your parish pew. You might also bring your drawings or a photo of your whole family with you to Mass and pray for them in your pew.

Finish your prayer time with the following Scripture passage, which we used to introduce the book you are reading. We pray that it means much more to you now than when you began reading this book. God is faithful!

Do not fear, for I have redeemed you;
    I have called you by name, you are mine.
When you pass through the waters, I will be with you;
    and through the rivers, they shall not overwhelm you;
when you walk through fire you shall not be burned,
    and the flame shall not consume you. . . .
Because you are precious in my sight,
    and honored, and I love you,
I give people in return for you,
    nations in exchange for your life.
Do not fear, for I am with you;
    I will bring your offspring from the east,
    and from the west I will gather you, . . .
everyone who is called by my name,
    whom I created for my glory,
    whom I formed and made.
(Isaiah 43:1-2, 4-5, 7)

Resources

Websites

www.bustedhalo.com. Paulist Young Adult Ministries, 405 W. 59th St., New York, NY. Addresses questions such as these: What role does spirituality play in life? How do we find work that feeds the soul? How do we remain moral in this crazy world?

www.christkey.com. Authors' website addressing a broad range of spiritual needs, links to additional websites, and resources for reaching inactive Catholics at www.catholicevangeler.com and www.christmascarolfestival.com.

www.ncyama.org. National Catholic Young Adult Ministry Association, 415 Michigan Avenue, NE, Suite 40, Washington, DC 20017-4503. E-mail: info@ncyama.org. The National Catholic Young Adult Ministry Association helps those who minister to young adult Catholics (late teens, twenties, and thirties).

www.OnceCatholic.org. St. Anthony Messenger Press, 1615 Republic St., Cincinnati, OH 45210. Puts inactive Catholics in touch with a face-to-face community of Catholics. Walks a person through their issues with the Church.

www.renewtot.org. Theology on Tap, RENEW International, 1232 George Street, Plainfield, NJ 07062-1717. Program promoting spiritual growth for Catholic adults in their twenties and thirties. Includes young-adult planned speaker series in local bars or restaurants featuring food, drink, and theological discussion.

www.osv.com, Our Sunday Visitor's Catholic Guide to the Internet: (www.osv.com/LinkClick.aspx?fileticket=0IoiMtYlYHQ%3d&tabid=7621). Readers' choices for best Catholic apps, spirituality, community building, news, and resources.

Books for Adults in Their Twenties and Thirties

Hendey, Lisa M. *Handbook for Catholic Moms: Nurturing Your Heart, Mind, Body, and Soul.* Notre Dame, IN: Ave Maria Press, 2010. For moms of school-age children. Many more resources are available at www.catholicmoms.com.

Hoover, Brett C. *Losing Your Religion, Finding Your Faith: Spirituality and Young Adults.* Mahwah, NJ: Paulist Press, 1998. Describes the lifelong process of discovering both God and self—faith can grow only when religion is doubted, lost, and found again in a new light.

Langford, Jeremy. *God Moments: Why Faith Really Matters for a New Generation.* Maryknoll, NY: Orbis Books, 2001. Addresses spiritual seekers.

Locklin, Reid B. *Spiritual But Not Religious? An Oar Stroke Closer to the Farther Shore.* Collegeville, MN: Liturgical Press,

2005. A conversation with young adults that views the Christian Church as a raft—not an obstacle—on the journey to the farther spiritual shore.

Muldoon, Tim. *Come to the Banquet: Nourishing Our Spiritual Hunger.* Plymouth, UK: Sheed & Ward, 2002. A book aimed at young adult seekers showing how the Christian spiritual tradition can nourish them.

Pierce, Gregory F. *A Spirituality at Work: 10 Ways to Balance Your Life on the Job.* Chicago, IL: Loyola Press, 2001. Young adult guide for working, regardless of a person's job, location, or tasks. How to balance life and work, home and office, as well as your Catholic faith.

Ministering to Adults in Their Twenties and Thirties

Boucher, John and Therese. *When You Notice the Empty Pews: Simple Ways to Share Our Faith.* Princeton, NJ: www.catholicevangelizer.com, 2008. Website: www.christkey.com. Noticing empty pews can be the beginning of a call to share faith in sensitive but deliberate ways. You can do it through prayer, care, share, and dare to invite.

Carroll, Colleen. *The New Faithful: Why Young Adults Are Embracing Christian Orthodoxy.* Chicago, IL: Loyola Press, 2002. Analysis of young adults who are finding Jesus Christ and a spiritual home in vibrant parishes and churches.

Connecting Young Adults to Catholic Parishes: Best Practices in Catholic Young Adult Ministry. Washington, DC: USCCB Publishing, 2010. 800-235-8722, www.usccbpublishing.org. How to draw young adults who already have contact with us into the life of the parish community.

Cusick, Fr. John and Katherine DeVries. *The Basic Guide to Young Adult Ministry.* Maryknoll, NY: Orbis Books, 2001. Program for ministering to and with young adults that is filled with sound principles and effective strategies.

Duquin, Lorene Hanley. *When a Loved One Leaves the Church: What You Can Do.* Huntington, IN: Our Sunday Visitor, 2001. Commonsense answers for those who are troubled about loved ones.

Eldredge, Becky. "Calling the Next Generation of Catholic Evangelizers," *Evangelization Exchange,* October 2010. Paulist Evangelization Ministries, Washington, DC. Available online at http://pemdc.org/ee1010–eldredge-handout/. Eight hungers in young adults provide opportunities for them to become the next generation of Catholic evangelizers.

Go and Make Disciples: A *National Plan and Strategy for Catholic Evangelization in the United States.* [English and Spanish] Washington, DC: USCCB Publishing, 2002. 800-235-8722, www.usccbpublishing.org. Available online at http://www.usccb.org/beliefs-and-teachings/how-we-teach/evangelization/go-and-make-disciples/go-and-make-disciples-a-national-plan

-and-strategy-for-catholic-evangelization-in-the-united-states.
cfm. Discover how the Spirit is leading you to evangelize and
how this can reshape our parishes and our institutions.

Hoge, Dean R., William D. Dinges, and Mary Johnson. *Young
Adult Catholics: Religion in a Culture of Choice.* Notre Dame,
IN: University of Notre Dame Press, 2001. Effective ministry
to young adults depends on understanding their attitudes and
the needs of the current generation of Catholics in their twenties and thirties.

John Paul II, "Internet: A New Forum for Proclaiming the Gospel," 36th World Communications Day, 2002. Available online
at http://www.vatican.va/holy_father/john_paul_ii/messages/
communications/documents/hf_jp-ii_mes_20020122_world
-communications-day_en.html. For the Church, the new world
of cyberspace is a summons to the great adventure of using the
potential of the Internet to proclaim the gospel message.

Muldoon, Tim. *Seeds of Hope: Young Adults and the Catholic
Church in the United States.* Mahwah, NJ: Paulist Press, 2008.
Asks what kind of church we are inviting young people to join
and analyzes the contemporary social and ecclesial landscapes
for signs of hope for the future of the Church.

*Sons and Daughters of the Light: A Pastoral Plan for Minis-
try with Young Adults.* Washington, DC: USCCB Publishing,
1997. 800-235-8722, www.usccbpublishing.org. Available
online at http://old.usccb.org/laity/ygadult/toc.shtml. Pastoral

plan to encourage parishes and dioceses to recognize, support, and motivate ministry with, by, and for young adults.

Books for Parents of Young Adults

Boucher, Therese. *A Prayer Journal for Baptism in the Holy Spirit*. Locust Grove, VA: National Service Committee, 2000. Available online at www.renewed-life.com/shop/index.cfm. A forty-day prayer book for getting in touch with the graces of Baptism through daily Scriptures passages, including space for daily notes.

Fulwiler, Jennifer. *Being Present: What Technology Cannot Replace* (pamphlet). Huntingdon, IN: Our Sunday Visitor, 2010. Helpful guidelines for media and Internet use and sharing.

Guntzelman, Joan. *Surrendering Our Stress: Prayers to Calm the Soul and Strengthen the Spirit*. Frederick, MD: The Word Among Us Press, 2009. The prayers in this book will help you surrender your stress—and yourself—into the arms of God.

MacNutt, Frances. *The Practice of Healing Prayer: A How-to Guide for Catholics*. Frederick, MD: The Word Among Us Press, 2010. Step-by-step guide for how to pray with others; explains the various types of healings that we can expect— physical, emotional, spiritual; discusses the healing effects of the sacraments.

Koenig-Bricker, Woodeene. *Asking God for the Gifts He Wants to Give You.* Frederick, MD: The Word Among Us Press, 2008. Explains St. Alphonsus Liguori's advice in asking for forgiveness, wisdom, a share in divine love, confidence in the merits of Jesus and the intercession of Mary, and perseverance.

Chiffolo, Anthony E. *At Prayer with the Saints.* Liguori, MO: Ligouri Publications, 1998. Collection of saints' prayers suitable for adoration, sorrow, petition, and thanksgiving.

Vogt, Susan V. *Parenting Your Adult Child: Keeping the Faith (and Your Sanity).* Cincinnati, OH: St. Anthony Messenger Press, 2011. How to develop virtues that help parents respect and nurture the faith that lies deep within each young adult, no matter what it looks like on the surface.

Endnotes

1. Unless otherwise noted, saints' quotes are from *Living with Christ* (New London, CT: Bayard, Inc.).

2. Roger Zielke, *Blessed Marie of the Incarnation*, http://www.sspx.ca/Communicantes/Sep2004/Those_Who_Truly_Live.htm.

3. *A Follower of Francis*, "Solanus Casey: A Man Full of Thanks!" in *A Follower of Francis*, a blog by a secular Franciscan, http://paxchristirochester.blogspot.com/2010/11/solanus-casey-man-full-of-thanks.html.

4. Jill Haak Adels, *The Wisdom of the Saints: An Anthology* (New York: Oxford University Press, 1987), 55.

5. Ronda De Sola Chervin, *Quotable Saints* (Ann Arbor, MI: Servant Books, 1992), 211–212.

6. Right Rev. Robert Seton, D.D, ed., *Memoir, Letters, and Journal of Elizabeth Seton, Convert to the Catholic Faith and Sister of Charity,* volume II (New York: P. O'Shae, 1869), 257.

7. Ibid., 262.

8. Robert J. Morgan, *He Shall Be Called* (New York: Time Warner, 2005), 152–153.

9. "The Question of God," Corrie ten Boom, http://www.pbs.org/wgbh/questionofgod/voices/boom.html.

10. Blessed John Paul II, *Dives in Misericordia* (On the Mercy of God), Encyclical Letter, November 30, 1980, 13, accessed at www.vatican.va./holy_father/john_paul_ii/encyclicals/documents/hf_jp-ii_enc_30111980_dives-in-misericordia_en.html.

11. Mary Lou Quinlan, "Mom's Secret Weapon: the God Box," RealSimple.com, November 12, 2010, (http://www .cnn.com/2010/LIVING/11/12/rs.inside.god.box/index .html?hpt=Sbin.)

12. "Edith Stein: Living under the Mystery of the Cross," accessed at the website of *The Word Among Us*, http://wau.org/ resources/article/st_edith_stein/.

13. Bert Ghezzi, *Voices of the Saints* (New York: Doubleday, 2000), 335.

14. *Sons and Daughters of the Light: A Pastoral Plan for Ministry with Young Adults* (Washington, DC: USCCB Publishing, March 2010), preface, accessed at http://old.usccb.org/laity/ ygadult/toc.shtml.

15. *Sacraments Today: Belief and Practice Among U.S. Catholics—Executive Summary 2008*, cara.georgetown .edu/sacraments.html.

16. *Sons and Daughters of the Light,* preface.

17. Blessed John Paul II, *Redemptoris Missio*, (Mission of the Redeemer), Encyclical Letter, December 7, 1990, 38, accessed at www.vatican.va/holy_father/john_paul_ii/encyclicals /documents/hf-jp-ii_enc_07121990_redemptoris-missio .en.html.

18. Bernard Lonergan and several other authors.

19. Ronald Rolheiser, OMI, "Touching Our Loved One inside the Body of Christ," *Evangelization Exchange*, www.pncea.org, June–July 2010.

20. Becky Eldredge, "Calling the Next Generation of Catholic Evangelizers," *Evangelization Exchange*, www. pncea.org, October 2010. See Eldredge's blog at http:// everythingisholynow.blogspot.com.

21. Pope Benedict XVI, Message for the 45th World Communications Day, June 5, 2011, accessed at www .vatican.va/holy_father/benedict_xvi/messages /communications/documents/hf_ben-xvi_mes_20110124_45th -world-communicatons-day_en.html.

22. "How Technology Is Influencing Families," Barna Group, May 23, 2011, accessed at http://www.barna.org/family-kids -articles/488-how-technology-is-influencing-families.

23. "Pope Chats to Astronauts in Space," Vatican Radio, May 21, 2011, accessed at www.radiovaticana.org/en1/articolo .asp?c=489185.

24. Blessed Pope John Paul II, "Internet: A New Forum for Proclaiming the Gospel," 36th World Communication Day, May 12, 2002, accessed at www.vatican.va/holy_father/john _paul_ii/messages/communications/documents/ hf_jp-ii_mes_20020122_world-communications-day_en.html.

25. St. Ambrose, *Expl. symb.* 1:PL 17, 1193, quoted in the *Catechism of the Catholic Church*, 197.

26. Randy Sprinkler, *Follow Me* (Birmingham AL: New Hope, 2001), 85.

27. Anthony F. Chiffolo, *At Prayer with the Saints* (Liguori, MO: Liguori Publications, 1998), 192.

28. Edward Schillebeeckx, OP, *God Is New Each Moment* (New York: Seabury, 1983), 108.

29. Therese Boucher, *A Prayer Journal for Baptism in the Holy Spirit* (Locust Grove, VA: National Service Committee, 2002), 7.

30. "The Wisdom of the Saints," accessed at http://www.catholic-forum.com/churches/cathteach/quotes_saints.htm.

31. Jill Haak Adels, 74.

32. Susan V. Vogt, *Parenting Your Adult Child* (Cincinnati, OH: St. Anthony Messenger Press, 2011), 118.

33. CBS News, "The Royal Wedding," April 29, 2011, accessed at http://www.cbsnews.com/8301-32917_162-20058538-10391716.html.

34. John Cumming, ed., *Letters from Saints to Sinners* (New York: Crossroad Publishing Company), 158.

35. Michael J. Miller, "Joseph Moscati: Saint, Doctor, and Miracle Worker." *Lay Witness*, March/April 2004, accessed at http://www.catholiceducation.org/articles/catholic_stories/cs0067.html.

36. Anthony F. Chiffolo, 31.

37. Pope Benedict XVI, Christmas Address to the Roman Curia, December 22, 2008, accessed at http://www.vatican.va/holy_father/benedict_xvi/speeches/2008/december/documents/hf_ben-xvi_spe_20081222_curia-romana_en.html.

38. Robert Wuthnow, *After the Baby Boomers: How Twenty- and Thirty-Somethings Are Shaping the Future of American Religion* (Princeton, NJ: Princeton University Press, 2007), 13.

39. Patrick Ahern, *Maurice and Thérèse: The Story of a Love* (New York: Doubleday, 1998), 169.

40. John Henry Newman, *Discourses to Mixed Congregations.*

41. www.youtube.com/watch?v=0xwzItqYmII.

42. Ronald Dunn, *Don't Just Stand There, Pray Something: The Incredible Power of Intercessory Prayer* (Nashville: Thomas Nelson Publishers, 1992), 20.

43. Ronda De Sola Chervin, 127.

44. Ronald Dunn, 73.

45. For lists and biographies of saints who were married and/or parents, read Joan Carroll Cruz, *Secular Saints* (Rockford, IL: Tan Books and Publishing, 1989), 757.

46. Woodeene Koenig-Bricker, *Praying with the Saints* (Chicago: Loyola Press, 2001), 233.

47. John and Therese Boucher, *When You Notice the Empty Pews: Simple Ways to Share Our Faith* (Princeton, NJ: www.catholicevangelizer.com, 2008), 6–10.

48. Pope Benedict XVI, *Verbum Domini* (On the Word of God in the Life and Mission of the Church), Post-Synodal Apostolic Exhortation, September 30, 2010, 91, accessed at http://www.vatican.va/holy_father/benedict_xvi/apost_exhortations/documents/hf_ben-xvi_exh_20100930_verbum-domini_en.html.

the WORD
among us®
The *Spirit* of Catholic Living

This book was published by The Word Among Us. Since 1981, The Word Among Us has been answering the call of the Second Vatican Council to help Catholic laypeople encounter Christ in the Scriptures.

The name of our company comes from the prologue to the Gospel of John and reflects the vision and purpose of all of our publications: to be an instrument of the Spirit, whose desire is to manifest Jesus' presence in and to the children of God. In this way, we hope to contribute to the Church's ongoing mission of proclaiming the gospel to the world so that all people would know the love and mercy of our Lord and grow ever more deeply in love with him.

Our monthly devotional magazine, *The Word Among Us*, features meditations on the daily and Sunday Mass readings, and currently reaches more than one million Catholics in North America and another half million Catholics in one hundred countries around the world. Our book division, The Word Among Us Press, publishes numerous books, Bible studies, and pamphlets that help Catholics grow in their faith.

To learn more about who we are and what we publish, log on to our website at www.wau.org. There you will find a variety of Catholic resources that will help you grow in your faith.

Embrace His Word, Listen to God . . .

www.wau.org